CHRISTIANITY

AND

WORLD RELIGIONS

E. Luther Copeland

Convention Press

NASHVILLE   **TENNESSEE**

© 1963 • CONVENTION PRESS
Nashville, Tennessee

5110–01

Code Number: Church Study Course
This book is number 1001 in category 10, section
for Adults and Young People

Library of Congress Catalog Card Number: 63–8378
Printed in the United States of America
175. o 62 R.R.D.

Contents

About the Author

THE AUTHOR of this book, Edwin Luther Copeland, is professor of missions at Southeastern Baptist Theological Seminary, Wake Forest, North Carolina. Prior to accepting that place of service, Dr. Copeland was a Southern Baptist missionary to Japan (1948 to 1956). He taught at Seinan Gakuin in Fukuoka and served as president of that institution.

Born in Drennen, Nicholas County, West Virginia, Dr. Copeland attended elementary and high school there. After working seven years in the lumber business, he answered the call to preach which he had sensed as a child and which was newly impressed on him. He entered Mars Hill College, North Carolina, to begin preparation, and from Mars Hill he went to Furman University, where he was graduated in 1944, magna cum laude. He holds a Th. M. degree from Southern Baptist Theological Seminary (1946) and Ph. D. from Yale University (1949).

For the Foreign Affairs Association of Japan in 1954, Dr. Copeland wrote the monograph, *The Japanese Government and Protestant Christianity, 1889–1900.*

He is active in the American Society of Church History, and is a member of the Executive Committee of the American Association of Missions Professors.

Dr. and Mrs. Copeland (the former Louise Tadlock of Tahlequah, Oklahoma) have four daughters and one son.

Church Study Course

THE CHURCH STUDY COURSE began October 1, 1959. It is a merger of three courses previously promoted by the Sunday School Board —the Sunday School Training Course, the Graded Training Union Study Course, and the Church Music Training Course. On October 1, 1961, the Woman's Missionary Union principles and methods studies were added.

The course is fully graded. The system of awards provides a series of five diplomas of twenty books each for Adults or Young People, two diplomas of five books each for Intermediates, and two diplomas of five books each for Juniors. Book awards earned previously in the Sunday School Training Course, the Graded Training Union Study Course, and the Church Music Training Course may be transferred to the new course.

The course is comprehensive, with books grouped into twenty categories. The purpose of the course is to help Christians to grow in knowledge and conviction, to help them to grow toward maturity in Christian character and competence for service, to encourage them to participate worthily as workers in their churches, and to develop leaders for all phases of church life and work.

The Church Study Course is promoted by the Baptist Sunday School Board, 127 Ninth Avenue, North, Nashville, Tennessee, through its Sunday School, Training Union, Church Music, and Church Administration departments; and the Woman's Missionary Union, 600 North Twentieth Street, Birmingham, Alabama; and by the respective departments in the states affiliated with the Southern Baptist Convention. A description of the course and the system of awards may be found in the leaflet "Trained Workmen" which may be obtained without charge from any one of the departments named.

A record of all awards earned should be maintained in each church. A person should be designated by the church to keep the files. Forms for such records may be ordered from any Baptist Book Store.

Requirements for Credit in Class
or Home Study

If CREDIT is desired for the study of this book in a class or by home study, the following requirements must be met:

I. In Classwork

1. The class must meet a minimum of seven and one-half clock hours. The required time does not include assembly periods. Ten class periods of forty-five minutes each are recommended. (If laboratory or clinical work is desired in specialized or technical courses, this requirement may be met by six clock hours of classwork and three clock hours of supervised laboratory or clinical work.)

2. A class member who attends all class sessions and completes the reading of the book within a week following the last class session will not be required to do any written work for credit.

3. A class member who is absent from one or more sessions must answer the questions (pp. 156–157) on all chapters he misses. In such a case, he must turn in his paper within a week, and he must certify that he has read the book.

4. The teacher should request an award for himself. A person who teaches a book in the section for Intermediates or Juniors (any category) or conducts an approved unit of instruction for Nursery, Beginner, or Primary children will be granted an award in category 11, Special Studies, which will count as an elective on his own diploma. He should specify in his request the name of the book taught, or the unit conducted for Nursery, Beginner, or Primary children.

5. The teacher should complete the "Request for Book Awards —Class Study" (Form 150) and forward it within two weeks after the completion of the class to the Church Study Course Awards Office, 127 Ninth Avenue, North, Nashville 3, Tennessee.

II. In Home Study

1. A person who does not attend any class session may receive credit by answering all questions for written work as indicated in the book (pp. 156–157). When a person turns in his paper on home study, he must certify that he has read the book.

2. Students may find profit in studying the text together, but individual papers are required. Carbon copies or duplicates in any form cannot be accepted.

3. Home study work papers may be graded by the pastor or a person designated by him, or they may be sent to the Church Study Course Awards Office for grading. The form entitled "Request for Book Awards—Home Study" (Form 151) must be used in requesting awards. It should be mailed to the Church Study Course Awards Office, 127 Ninth Avenue, North, Nashville 3, Tennessee.

III. CREDIT FOR THIS BOOK

This book is number 1001 in category 10 section for Adults and Young People.

STATISTICS ON WORLD RELIGIONS [1]

Christians 854,000,000
    Protestant and Anglican........263,700,000
    Orthodox and Eastern.......... 96,700,000
    Roman Catholic 493,600,000
Jews 12,800,000
Moslems 366,000,000
Buddhists 186,000,000
Hindus 316,000,000
Confucians ....300,000,000 [2]
Taoists .... 30,000,000 [2]
Sikhs 6,200,000
Jains 1,600,000
Parsees (Zoroastrians) 128,000
Shintoists 34,500,000
Animists (Primitive Religion).................124,000,000 [3]

---

[1] Adapted from *World Christian Handbook*, 1962 edition (London: World Dominion Press, 1962), pp. 237–251.

[2] These figures on Chinese religions are quite unrealistic.

[3] *Occasional Bulletin* from the Missionary Research Library, May 6, 1958, p. 2.

CHAPTER 1 OUTLINE

RELIGION AND RELIGIONS

I. TOWARD A DEFINITION OF RELIGION

II. THE UNIVERSALITY OF RELIGION

III. THE ORIGIN OF RELIGION
1. Theories of the Origin of Religion
2. The Biblical Standpoint

IV. THE RELIGIOUS SITUATION IN TODAY'S WORLD
1. Secularism
2. Revival of Religions
3. The New Meeting of Christianity and Other Religions
4. The Challenge to Christians

1

Religion and Religions

THE GOSPEL of Jesus Christ appeared in a world of "many 'gods' and many 'lords' " (1 Cor. 8:5, RSV) and among people who were "very religious" (Acts 17:22, RSV). That was over nineteen hundred years ago, but people are yet very religious and have many religions. The gospel still calls men, whether they are religious or irreligious, humbly to accept the gift of God's redemption in Jesus Christ.

This chapter raises some questions about the nature of religion and then attempts to describe the religious situation in today's world.

I. TOWARD A DEFINITION OF RELIGION

What is religion? Perhaps most of us think we know the answer to this question until we attempt a definition. The fact is, however, that religion is not easy to define and that definitions vary widely, often reflecting the prejudices of those defining. One of the popular textbooks in world religions lists about twenty different definitions of religion—and these are but representative examples! [1]

Some definitions emphasize the emotional element of religion; some, the ethical content, some, the aspect of worship; and some, still other characteristics. E. D. Soper insists that:

"Religion consists of a number of elements. It makes a demand on the whole of man's life, intellect, emotion and will; it is both individual and social; it is worship, yet it is more than worship; it is all the values which give worth and meaning to human life. But at its core religion is always a relation-

1

ship, a conscious relation of human beings and God or higher powers, however they may be conceived." [2]

Perhaps this definition reflects Soper's Christian experience and viewpoint and is more ideal than real. Not all religions conserve "all the values which give worth and meaning to human life."

Viewed from the Christian standpoint, religion would certainly involve the knowledge of God by divine revelation. The Christian knows God as the self-existent source and sustainer of all existence. He knows God as the only perfect Being, the personal Lord who makes an absolute claim upon man while giving himself to man in Jesus Christ, the holy Companion who dwells within man, and the loving Father who unites men in one family. [3]

However, it is doubtful whether even Christians usually experience religion in this much wholeness. And it is certain, at least to Christians who know something of the history of religion, that this Christian understanding of religion represents a high-water mark of religion and revelation, which judges rather than describes religion as generally known.

How then can religion be defined more briefly and descriptively as common to all peoples? For this purpose it is difficult to improve upon the definition of William Newton Clarke: "Religion is the life of man in his superhuman relationships. . . ." [4] Or the statement of John B. Noss that "the basic feeling in all religion" is man's dependence upon something outside himself. [5]

II. The Universality of Religion

So far as we know, man is the only creature on this planet that has a religious consciousness. Not only is man uniquely religious, but he is also universally religious. This does not necessarily mean that every individual person is religious but that all peoples have a religion or religions. Archeology and history tell us that as far back as we have substantial traces of ancient man we also find evidences of his religion.

To be sure, some popular doctrines today deny religious faith, as, for example, communism. But it may be argued that communism itself is a kind of substitute religion; and, in any case, where communism has been dominant for a number of years or decades—which is especially true of Russia—it has been unable to eliminate religion. The universality of the religious consciousness in man is well established. Man seems to be incurably religious.

III. THE ORIGIN OF RELIGION

1. *Theories of the Origin of Religion*

When did religion begin? We may assume that religion originated with man. Scholars have constructed many theories of the origin of religion.

(1) *Evolutionary theories.*—Most of these theories are based upon the idea of evolution. They presuppose that for a while after man developed into what was truly human he had no religion, or that his religion was most simple and undeveloped. Only after a long development did his religion reach monotheism, the belief in one god.

These various theories find the origin of religion in different human emotions or desires. One of them proposes that perhaps religion began with a fear of ghosts, resulting in ancestor worship as early religion. Another says that maybe the belief in spirits or in a mysterious force inhabiting objects of the natural world came first. Again, another theory suggests that possibly the desire for a unified community life resulted in certain religious feelings and rites. Or, there may have been a sense of awe at life's deep mysteries, leading to an awareness of divine presence. And so the theories go. These theories usually see religion developing first into a primitive spirit worship, then into polytheism, the belief in many gods, and finally into monotheism, belief in one God.

(2) *The "Primitive Monotheism" theory.*—These theories of evolutionary development have been challenged. Scholars have found what they believe to be evidences or remnants of monotheism among modern primitives. Among many primitive tribes there is the concept of a "high-god" who is creator and source of the world. These presumed signs of monotheism have led some to believe that religion began in a recognition of the one God. Then, because of the Fall of man, it degenerated into polytheism, the belief in many gods, and other degraded forms of belief.

Critics of this "primitive monotheism" theory point out that the high-god is usually remote from the life of the people. Other gods are closer to the people, serving their immediate needs and receiving their worship and devotion. It could be answered, of course, that, because of man's Fall and alienation from the one God, one might expect that where there is some remembrance of him there would be also a sense of remoteness and separation.

It should be remembered, however, that today's "primitives" are still modern men with unknown ages of human history behind them. One may theorize if he wishes, and it is interesting and possibly helpful to do so. But the truth remains that, from the standpoint of history and science, no one can prove how religion began.

2. *The Biblical Standpoint*

Regardless of how man's religion may have begun, from the standpoint of biblical faith, man is religious because God created him for fellowship with him as his child. Man's religious consciousness is a part of the divine image in which man is created. This religious consciousness apprehends the revelation of God as disclosed in nature, society, and the inner life of man. But, being itself distorted by sin, man's religious consciousness perverts the truth of God's revelation. Thus, the many religions, having been shaped by the fallen nature of man, are at once products both of divine revelation and human perversion (see Rom. 1:18–25). This is true of religion as such, whenever it may have begun, and it is true of man's various religions, whenever they develop. Thus one may expect to meet with elements both of the divine and the demonic in religion, both of truth and falsity.

IV. The Religious Situation in Today's World

The religious development of man, as other aspects of his culture, has become increasingly complex. There are many religions and many substitutes for religion in the modern world. (See Statistics on World Religions on page VII.) Indeed, it appears that the present is a time of religious ferment unexcelled in human history.

1. *Secularism*

Strange as it may seem, today's revival of religious interest comes in an age of widespread secularism and irreligion. About thirty-five years ago, missionary strategists were being reminded that the greatest rival of Christianity was not the non-Christian religions but "a worldwide secular way of life and interpretation of the nature of things." [6]

What was meant by "secularism" was a manner of living or an interpretation of life that includes only the natural order of things and does not find God essential for life or thought. It simply leaves God out of account, though not necessarily denying his existence. Indeed, it may seek to use God and religion for human ends. At its worst, secularism is a concern for material things only. At its best, it seeks good for man while ignoring God. It tends to deny God and truth as ultimate values and to make absolute, relative values such as education, government, or science.

Secularism is a world movement which forms a new frontier for all religions. Even so-called "spiritual" nations such as India are permeated by secularism. Some of the new nationalisms are secularistic faiths that substitute the State for God. Communism is a secularistic religion in that, while denying God and religion, it demands for itself the kind of unconditional commitment and loyalty which only religion can require.

Secularism is exceedingly diverse and therefore exceedingly subtle. It is a many-sided paganism. It includes communism, but it also includes the vague materialism of American life whereby a man may conform to "religion" but actually be unaffected by vital faith and conviction, unconsciously giving himself to secular values. It includes the blurry attitude of many American churchgoers that any kind of religious belief, Christian or otherwise, is all right—because really none is important enough to be excited about! Or else because faith itself, rather than the Sovereign God, is the object of faith!

Another variety of secularism is scientism which looks upon science as a secular messiah that has outmoded all religion. This expression of secularism is very prevalent among college students in much of the world. Often in Japan this kind of statement comes from students: "My family are Buddhists, but I have no religion. I do not think religion has any place in a scientific age. Science has outmoded all religion." And this seems to be an attitude found in varying measure throughout the world.

2. Revival of Religions

While secularism continues today as a formidable rival for Christianity and other religions everywhere, it is yet true that this is a time of revival of the non-Christian religions. Not many years ago it was common for Christians in contact with other religions—especially Christian missionaries—to say that these religions were in a dying state and would soon become extinct. It was supposed that these religions would find no way of adjustment to a secular and scientific world and therefore would not be able to survive.

The situation now is very different. The great world religions, particularly Islam, Hinduism, and Buddhism, are experiencing revival. Though these faiths have many unsolved problems concerning the harmonizing of their essential beliefs with the modern world, they have taken a new lease on life and are manifesting considerable vitality.

In large part this revival of religions is dependent upon nationalistic and cultural revival. The newly independent nations of the East have a new self-consciousness and awareness of their own significance and destiny. They are giving strong emphasis to their unique cultural heritages and national traditions. In this situation, their own religions are receiving renewed appreciation and emphasis as vital and essential elements of the national character. This is true, for instance, of Hinduism in India, Buddhism in Burma, and Islam in the Near Eastern countries.

Closely related to the revival of nationalism today is a spirit of reaction against the West and against Christianity and an attempt to counteract the influence of Christian missions. This spirit is, at least in part, responsible for the missionary activity of some of the non-Christian religions.

Until recently Islam spread by means of unorganized lay missionary work. In its early history it accompanied military and commercial expansion. Now Islam is organizing missions in an attempt especially to win Africa to the Moslem faith. And it is registering notable successes. In addition, the Ahmadiyya sect of Islam is sending missionaries to the United States and Europe.

Buddhists also, for the first time in history, have organized missions to the Western world. Likewise, centers of Hindu missionary propaganda may be found in the large cities of our own country and Europe.

More will be said of the missions of the non-Christian religions later. Suffice it to say at this point that they are due more to Christian influence than to inherent missionary conviction. They represent movements of resistance to the Christian mission in non-Christian nations.

Nevertheless, it would be a mistake to view the revival of non-Christian faiths as due solely to the secondary or negative motives of nationalism and anti-Christian reaction. There must be also something of positive religious dynamic, though this may be difficult to separate from the non-religious impulses. A new sense of maturity can be discerned, at least in the thinking of some of the adherents of the non-Christian religions. Their thought is something like this:

"Our religion has stood face to face with the West for a long time. We have heard the preaching of Christianity and have observed its missionaries at work among us for a century or more. We have studied Western history and philosophy in our schools, and we have seen science and technology and the various ideologies of Europe and America flooding into our country.

"We have felt the tremendous impact of modern thought upon our ancient culture and religion. But our religion has not surrendered. It has found ways of adjustment and will continue to do so. Its real nature has not been destroyed or significantly altered. So we stand with new confidence as members of a mature religion which has a message not only for our country but for the world."

3. *The New Meeting of Christianity and Other Religions*

New missionary activity of the non-Christian religions combines with the unprecedented intermingling of cultures today to produce a new meeting of Christianity with the other religions.

A very important factor in this new meeting toward which the religions are heading is the existence of the so-called younger churches. These are the Christian churches which have been planted in almost every nation by modern missions. Although numerically small and weak in many places, churches do exist. They are planted in the soil of non-Christian cultures, and face the members of the other faiths as fellow citizens and fellow sharers in a cultural heritage. This worldwide fellowship of Christians, called by William Temple "the great new fact of our era," is of inestimable significance.

Another mark of the new meeting of religions is the end of the one-way traffic of Christian missions to non-Christian lands. Now, as has already been pointed out, there is the two-way street which includes missions from them to us. And no doubt this reverse traffic of missions from non-Christian to Christian will increase. As yet, these missions are not of significant proportions.

These formal missionary activities of non-Christians to Christian lands should cause concern. Yet, the cultures of the East, including their religions, are exerting their influence in our society in much more extensive and diverse ways. Americans traveling and residing abroad, tourists from other countries visiting the United States, immigrants coming to live among us, exchange of professors and students—all of these bring to us knowledge of the non-Christian religions. And the modern media of mass communication—radio, television, the press, movies—serve to multiply many times the effectiveness of their propaganda.

Add to this contradictory pattern of secularistic and religious revival, the birth and development of new sects and religions in many countries. A picture emerges of tremendous religious diversity and activity, even in a secular age.

Secular faiths, as well as bona fide religions, are competing for the loyalty and devotion of the world's people. Their voices demand the commitment of men and women to something less than the God and Father of our Lord Jesus Christ. And their voices are loud and constant.

4. *The Challenge to Christians*

These competing religious claims constitute a challenge to Christian conviction. Christians must be sure that their unconditional loyalty and commitment are given to Jesus Christ. This is no time for halfhearted commitment. There are flaming faiths in the world today with devotees fanatically convinced that what they believe is right. Any religion which does not believe in its own unique worth and the necessity of its propagation cannot hope to survive, much less accomplish a world mission.

It is also imperative that Christians study the non-Christian religions. It is especially essential that missionaries have a deep understanding of these systems of faith and life. But it is increasingly important for all of us in America who are concerned with the propagation of the gospel to know something about the non-Christian religions. This is because of the growing prominence of non-Christian religious propaganda here.

This book is a modest attempt to contribute to this needed understanding.

FOR CLASS DISCUSSION

1. Make your own definitions of "religion" and of "Christianity."
2. What is "secularism"? Give some examples of secularism in our society.
3. Cite evidences of religious revival in the world today. What are some reasons for this revival?

NOTES

[1] Edmund Davison Soper, *The Religions of Mankind*, third edition, revised (New York: Abingdon-Cokesbury Press, 1951), pp. 13–20. Used by permission of Abingdon Press.

[2] *Ibid.*, p. 19.

[3] Herbert H. Farmer, *Revelation and Religion* (New York: Harper and Brothers, 1954), pp. 78–79.

[4] William Newton Clarke, *An Outline of Christian Theology* (New York: Charles Scribner's Sons, 1898), p. 1. Used by permission of Charles Scribner's Sons.

[5] John B. Noss, *Man's Religions*, revised edition (New York: The Macmillan Company, 1956), p. 3. Used with the permission of the Macmillan Company.

[6] Rufus M. Jones, "Secular Civilization and the Christian Task," *The Jerusalem Meeting of the International Missionary Council* (New York: International Missionary Council, 1928, 8 vols.), Vol. I, p. 230. Used by permission of the Division of World Mission and Evangelism, World Council of Churches.

PRIMITIVE RELIGION

I. PRIMITIVE PEOPLES AND PRIMITIVE RELIGION

II. THE GENERAL CHARACTERISTICS OF PRIMITIVE RELIGION

1. Belief in Mana
2. Animism
3. Polytheism
4. Magic
5. Tabu
6. Purification Rites
7. Sacrifice
8. Prayer
9. Totemism
10. Mythology

III. PRIMITIVE RELIGION ILLUSTRATED: THE AINU OF JAPAN

IV. CHRISTIANITY AND PRIMITIVE RELIGION TODAY

2

Primitive Religion

THIS CHAPTER attempts to describe the religion of the millions of people in the world who are called "primitive." It also includes an evaluation of their religion from the Christian standpoint.

I. PRIMITIVE PEOPLES AND PRIMITIVE RELIGION

It has already been suggested that when we speak of "primitive religion" today we are not referring to the religion of the earliest human beings. We are talking, for the most part, about the religion of certain people who are living today.

"Primitive" here, therefore, refers not to time but to type of culture. The people whose religion we are discussing have a very simple material culture. Usually, they cannot read or write. In general, they still retain their Stone Age religion while accepting certain aspects of modern civilization.

Primitive people, in this understanding of the word, are found in both hemispheres and in many countries. Examples are various Negro and Negroid tribes of Africa, the Ainu of Japan, some hill tribes of India, and Eskimos; and also aboriginal Indian tribes of the Americas. But, of course, some Indians had reached a high level of civilization by the fifteenth century when they were discovered and exploited by the white man.

For various reasons, including their wide distribution, the number of primitive people in the world is quite difficult to estimate. Statistics vary widely. A recent survey gives a figure of 124,000,000.[1]

Primitive religion is sometimes called "animism," a term meaning belief in spirits. Another name which is sometimes used is "tribal religion." However, in this discussion the term "primitive religion" will be used because this is more commonly used and therefore, perhaps, less confusing.

Let it be quite clear, however, that the term "primitive" is not meant to imply mental inferiority. Until recently even in scholarly writings on primitive religion, it was often assumed that the mental ability of primitive people was by nature different from and inferior to that of modern "civilized" man. The primitive, it was supposed, represented a lower stage in human evolution, and had a "child mind" or a "prelogical" mind. This mistaken notion still persists, even in writings on primitive religion. No doubt the common attitude among those who are not acquainted with the scientific study of man called anthropology is to view the primitives as mentally inferior.

To be sure, primitive people think differently from so-called civilized man. But anthropologists have shown that this difference is not due to a lack in mental ability but to the cultural and social environment which conditions the thought processes of primitive man.

The characteristic mental attitude of primitive people is sometimes called "primitive credulity." That is, primitive man lives in the world of sensory experience. He is not often critical of his sensations. Rather, he takes them at face value. This uncritical attitude leads to some fantastic notions. All sorts of ideas are true to the primitive because his senses tell him that they are true. "What seems real is real." [2]

One would expect, therefore, that the religion of primitives would be marked by a great deal of superstition and simplicity when compared with ours. They have no sacred scriptures, for most of them have no written language. Usually they are without well-built temples and monuments, because many of them do not have permanently settled homes. Yet they do have well-defined religious traditions, beliefs, and rituals which are passed on from generation to generation by word of mouth.

Moreover, it is well to remember that, however unscientific and superstitious the beliefs and practices of primitives may appear to us, those beliefs are held in the highest importance to them. And well they might be, for their religion, though exceedingly defective, has provided these tribal folk with social unity, with patterns of ethical behavior, and with some sense of security.

II. THE GENERAL CHARACTERISTICS OF PRIMITIVE RELIGION

1. *Belief in Mana*

Common to primitive folk everywhere is a belief in what scholars of religion call *mana,* from a term used by certain Pacific islanders. This is the belief in an unseen but powerful force in the world which manifests itself mysteriously in certain objects to give them uncommon excellence or power. It may be observed in the inanimate objects of nature but is most apt to assert itself in animals and persons. It may be transferred from one person or thing to another and it may be productive either of good or evil.

Possibly this belief arises from the mysterious happenings of the natural world. When a stone is loosened from the side of a precipice, striking and injuring somebody, it may seem to have mysterious power. Or, when one person appears immune to a plague or disease, he may appear to have some strange force in his body. At any rate, the belief in *mana* plays an important part in primitive religion. This is sometimes called "animatism" because it sees things as "animated" by some life-force. Among primitive peoples the belief in this mysterious power helps explain all events.

2. *Animism*

What is thought by many to be a refinement or advanced stage of animatism is animism, the belief in spiritual beings resident in persons and things. Most objects, inanimate as well as animate, are thought to possess their own individual spirits or souls, some of these being good and some evil.

If the world is thus peopled with powerful spirits, it is important to be on good terms with these spiritual beings. Hence the prevalence of spirit-worship. This is what is commonly called idolatry. Most anything may be worshiped by the primitive, depending on the recognition of power or spiritual presence within it: stones, especially those of unusual shape or those fashioned for implements or weapons; plants and trees, as representing the mysterious productivity of nature upon which man's life depends; and animals, which furnish man food and clothing and with which he feels kinship.

3. *Polytheism*

In primitive religion, animism tends to merge into polytheism, the belief in many gods. That is, spirit-worship is accompanied by the worship of deities who are more than the run-of-the-mill spiritual presences. Often these are gods of the water, air, fire, sky, and heavenly bodies. This worship is a recognition of the powers of the universe and their significance for man as a dependent being. Often some "high-god" is recognized as the father and ruler of the gods and creator of the universe. As noted earlier, this belief is thought by some scholars to be an evidence of a primitive revelation of the one God.

Here, then, are three varieties of belief and worship: animatism, animism, and polytheism. All three are characteristic of primitive religion, though the last, polytheism, is not usually well developed.

4. *Magic*

Very prominent in primitive religion are magic and the many beliefs and rites associated with it. Theoretically, and by definition, magic may be distinguished from religion. In religion, one seeks to bring himself into harmony with what he conceives to be of ultimate authority and significance. In magic, one attempts to use spiritual powers for his own ends.

Magic takes many forms. Natural magic is the use of devices which assume that the spirits react like people. An example is the beating of gongs to frighten the evil spirits away. Sympathetic or mimetic magic is based on the association of ideas. The rite performed is an imitation and anticipation of the result desired. An example: to obtain good results in hunting, a picture may be drawn in which an arrow pierces the hunted animal. There are many other categories of magic, including black magic or sorcery, in which one uses spirit-powers to injure other people.

"Shamanism" is a word derived from Siberian religion, but it refers to witch-doctors, medicine men, and such. Their equivalent in Siberian religion happens to be called a "shaman," and hence the term "shamanism." Shamanism is control over the spirits by a spirit-possessed individual, perhaps to bewitch people or to expel demons from them.

Another specialized practice of magic is fetishism. This makes use of the power in certain objects, called "fetishes," to exert influence on spiritual powers. Some objects, such as misshapen sticks, may possess power on their own. Others may be "charged" with power, possibly by a shaman.

5. *Tabu*

Obviously, magic is related to the concept of mana. So also is "tabu," another prominent feature of primitive religion. Because certain objects or persons are closely associated with mysterious power or spiritual presence, contact with them must be avoided. Common tabus are dead bodies, women in childbirth, blood, spittle, and many other items, depending upon the locality and tradition. The person of a chief is nearly always tabu, at least as long as he remains able to lead the tribe.

"More than one instance is on record of men and women who died of fright upon learning they had unwittingly eaten the remains of a chief's meal. Their bodies apparently could not survive so powerful a dosage of *mana*-imbued substance." [3]

6. *Purification Rites*

Purification rites are necessary to remove the pollution caused by tabu violations or other defilements. Washing in water or blood is a common means of purification; but there are many other, such as jumping through fire, fasting, shaving, and the like.

7. *Sacrifice*

An almost universal practice in primitive religion is sacrifice. This is the attempt through giving up something of value to attain or maintain a state of harmony with the spiritual powers. It may be that the attempt to placate an angry god is the primary idea behind sacrifice, but it is not the only motive. [4] Sacrifice goes beyond magic to a more purely religious impulse or at least to the recognition that some spiritual powers cannot be controlled, but only entreated.

8. *Prayer*

Thus prayer is associated with sacrifice, but not exclusively so. It may be a ritual prayer or incantation, the repetition of which may carry its own power. Or it may be the spontaneous utterance to some named or nameless power in a moment of danger and the dread of death. Usually, the prayer is intensely concerned with some human need. This fact is illustrated by a representative list of prayers of primitives compiled by Edwin A. Burtt, one of which, that of a Blackfoot Indian chief, follows:

"Great Sun Power! I am praying for my people, that they may be happy in the summer and that they may live through the cold of winter. Many are sick and in want. Pity them, and let them survive. Grant that they may live long and have abundance. . . .

"Great Spirit! Bless our children, friends and visitors through a happy life. May our trails lay straight and level before us. Let us live to be old. We are all your children, and we ask these things with good hearts." [5]

9. *Totemism*

Totemism, often found among primitives, is the association of the tribe with an animal (or occasionally a plant) as a mark or symbol of the social unity and identity of the tribe. "Totem" is a word from an American Indian tribe and means "group." Totemism may reflect the sense of man's intimate relationship to other categories of creation, either by resemblance or dependence. That is, the tribe may feel that its totem animal, by its courage or cunning or some other trait, represents the character of the tribe. Or, the animal may be a present or past chief source of food for the tribe.

10. *Mythology*

Primitive religion, in common with higher religions, abounds in mythology. This is the production and elaboration of stories to explain the meanings of things. Myths spring from the imagination or the dreams of primitive man or from both. Repetition of these stories may elaborate them or give them more satisfactory interpretations to answer puzzling questions.

Whether the myths are literally true is quite beside the point. What matters is whether they communicate to the primitive a spiritual truth or bring to him a psychological satisfaction. Actually, sometimes the myth-makers hit upon (or have a revelation of?) a profound truth; as, for example, the myth of an Indonesian tribe, re-enacted repeatedly in tribal ritual, that the life of the world depends upon the sacrifice and death of a god.[6]

III. PRIMITIVE RELIGION ILLUSTRATED: THE AINU OF JAPAN

The Ainu are classified as a "proto-Caucasian" people, meaning that they represent an ancient strand of what developed into the so-called white race. It is thought that they are more related, therefore, to modern Caucasians than to the Mongolian or yellow race.

They are an ancient people of Japan. Whether they are the very first people of that island country is debatable. At any rate, they were there when the present Japanese began to arrive, which was at least two thousand years ago. Where they are observed in their original racial stock, they are as different from the Japanese as is the American Indian from the white man. As a matter of fact, the two situations are somewhat parallel: the Japanese pushed the Ainu farther and farther to the north and the white man pushed the Indian westward. One difference is that the process in Japan was of much longer time span than that in America.

Physically, the Ainu are stocky, with large heads and shoulders. They are of dark complexion, but much more "white" than Mongoloid or brown. They do not believe in the necessity of bathing, and their open hearths keep their huts smoky, so actually they may not be as dark as they appear! The men are extremely hairy, another characteristic which distinguishes them from Mongolian peoples. The men wear heavy beards, and the women, not to be outdone, tattoo their upper lips to resemble a mustache.

Several scholars believe that the Ainu were at one time a numerous branch of the world's people, quite widespread in

eastern Asia, especially Siberia. They are reduced now, however, to dwindling minorities in Kamchatka, Sakhalin, the
Kurile Islands, and the northernmost of Japan's main islands,
Hokkaido. One recent estimate of their number is about
18,000.[7]

A contemporary description of the Ainu is tinged with
pathos. They are described as living in filth and poverty, 95
per cent of them having trachoma, 85 per cent tuberculosis,
and 75 per cent venereal disease![8] In addition, alcoholism is
very prevalent among them. Those who do not succumb to
these evils are being absorbed into the Japanese race. It is
predicted that within two more decades the pure Ainu stock
will have become extinct. One who visits their villages in
Hokkaido is struck with the tragedy of a disappearing people
whose culture is now a means of barter with tourists (they
sell their artistically carved wooden bears) and is fast becoming a museum piece.

As to religion, the Ainu manifest the familiar traits of
primitive religion as found elsewhere. They are animistic,
believing in good spirits opposed by demons. The Ainu are
also polytheistic. Their deities are numerous: gods and god-
desses of vegetation, of the atmosphere, of water, and of the
heavenly bodies. There is also a high-god distinguished from
all others as *Pase Kamui*, the "Chief God" or "True God" or
"God over all." The fire-god is quite important and is worshiped at the open hearth.

Magic, superstition, and tabus abound. Fetishism is highly
developed, in some of its aspects seeming to cross over from
the world of magic to that of worship. The common fetishes
are *inao*, carved from wood, with shavings turned down over
the stick and somewhat resembling a head of hair. The word
"*inao*" means "message-bearer" which fairly well describes
the fetish as a means of communication with the gods. There
is a household fetish, made of lilac wood and called the
"ancestral caretaker." It is used in fire worship and in the

offering of prayers to the dead. A guardian *inao* for the indi-
vidual is made of willow and inserted in a bundle of reeds.
Nusa are clusters of *inao*, often those that have been used.
They are inserted in the ground outside the house.

Cereal-worship is an interesting feature of Ainu religion.
Vegetation deities are worshiped with the proper rituals at
planting time. But at harvest time there are cereal offerings,
of the harvested grain, not only to the vegetation deities but
to the grain itself. Then the offering is eaten, presumably
signifying union with the deity or the receiving of the potency
of the deity.

Of all the ceremonies of the Ainu, the bear festival [9] is the
most fascinating, though marked by cruelty or sadism. A
bear, having been captured as a cub, is carefully nurtured
until it is at least a year old and fat. Then the owner invites
his friends to the festival, whereupon they make careful
preparations of their best clothes and ornaments and of festive cakes and millet dumplings.

After many hours of worship and merry dancing before
the bear's cage, the men arrange fetishes at a designated
place of worship. They then inform the bear that he is about
to be sent back to his ancestors in the mountains. He is reminded that if he is a good cub, he will reincarnate and return
to be honored as he is being honored at present. A worshipful
prayer in affectionate language is addressed to the bear.

After this ritual the bear is led out to the place of worship,
in tow by strong ropes, and then subjected to grueling torture
by shooting with blunt arrows. When the bear is thoroughly
enraged and the young braves are in a frenzy of excitement,
some of them rush in and kill the bear with an arrow or knife.
Strangling the bear has been outlawed by the Japanese
government. The blood is carefully caught and drunk by
some of the men while it is still warm.

The bear is then taken to a "fetish floor" inside the hut
where he is skinned and then beheaded. Offerings of food and

ornaments are made to the bear's head. Finally, after the bear's flesh is boiled and ready for eating, some of his own meat and broth and raw blood are offered to his head. When the bear has had time to eat (which leaves a great deal to the imagination!), the respectful silence is ended and the sacramental feasting is begun. The feast ends with the bear's head erected on a pole with some *nusa*—and with most everybody full of bear meat and rice wine and hilariously drunk!

In this way union with the totem animal is effected and the divine sustenance of the tribe, by the provision of meat, is insured.

IV. CHRISTIANITY AND PRIMITIVE RELIGION TODAY

There is much to be said for primitive religion as providing patterns of social and ethical behavior and giving a measure of order and stability to tribal society. It is true, also, that there are characteristics of primitive religion which are found in other religions, even in Christianity: worship, prayer, and sacrifice. Of course, these practices are often degraded in primitive religion.

Likewise, certain ideas and beliefs of primitives are generally considered true and are part of the religious heritage of man. Among these are belief in an after-life, some recognition of sin, and certain ethical ideals such as the value of love and sacrifice. In these beliefs and in the concept of high-gods, primitive religion preserves traces, at least, of original or general revelation. All this may be said in favor of primitive religion.

Yet there is much that is wrong, tragically wrong. Professor Soper has pointed out that the animist, or spirit-worshiper, is governed by fear more than by faith.[10] He has faith, but this is not the controlling attitude. He is surrounded by spirits of all kinds, many, if not most, of which are evil spirits bent on doing him harm. Fear is disorganizing and enslaving. So primitive man lives in bondage to fear and superstition.

"We are told that the most remarkable change which takes place in the experience of an animist when he becomes a Christian is the realization that he is living in a universe in which there is but one God and that this God is a God of love who cares for his people." [11]

It is assumed that a primitive civilization, when confronted continuously by a "higher" civilization, usually gives way to the latter. Under similar circumstances, primitive religion yields to a "higher" religion. However, two or three related facts should be recognized. One of these is that the transition from a primitive to a "modern" society does not usually come easily. It is often attended by a tragic disintegration of life and character. Another fact is that the meeting of primitives with moderns in today's world is often a meeting not with Christianity but with secularism. The consequence is an even more pathetic decomposition of life.

In Africa, for example, tribal structures are being shattered by the invasion of a secular, technological, and urban culture. One result is the breakup of family life and the degradation of personal character. In new situations, primitives seem more easily to preserve their superstitions and magic than their religion and morality.[12]

Some of us know, also, of the long series of tragedies which have befallen the American Indian in his relations with the white man. We are aware of the continuing pathos of those who try to live in the two worlds of Indian tribal life and American secular society. Too often they lose whatever sense they may have had of the meaning of life and turn to idleness and alcoholism.

Christians need to understand the social and psychological factors involved in the transition from a primitive to a more complex culture. These people who stand confused between two worlds must be helped not only to find a personal Saviour. They must be helped, also, to find a new community of faith and love which will enable them to live as whole persons in a complicated society.

FOR CLASS DISCUSSION

1. What is meant by "primitive religion"?
2. What are its general characteristics?
3. What is the definition for "magic"?
4. What should be the evangelistic approach to "primitive peoples"?

NOTES

[1] Cited in Frank W. Price, "World Christian and Missionary Statistics," *Occasional Bulletin* from the Missionary Research Library, IX:4 (May 6, 1958), p. 2. The category is "animism" rather than "primitive religion."

[2] John B. Noss, *Man's Religions*, revised edition (New York: The Macmillan Company, 1956), p. 13. Used by permission of The Macmillan Company.

[3] *Ibid.*, p. 18.

[4] Soper, *op. cit.*, p. 49.

[5] Edwin A. Burtt, *Man Seeks the Divine* (New York: Harper and Brothers, 1957), p. 42. Used by permission of Harper and Row, Publishers, Inc.

[6] Hendrik Kraemer, *Religion and the Christian Faith*. Published 1957, The Westminster Press. Used by permission.

[7] Carl Etter, *Ainu Folklore* (Chicago: Wilcox and Follett Company, 1949), p. 184.

[8] *Ibid.*, p. 205.

[9] See especially John Batchelor, *Ainu Life and Lore* (Tokyo: Kyobunkwan, 1926), Chapter XXVI.

[10] Edmund Davison Soper, *The Philosophy of the Christian World Mission* (New York: Abingdon Press, 1943), pp. 159 ff. Used by permission of Abingdon Press.

[11] *Ibid.*, p. 159.

[12] See Geoffrey Parrinder, *African Traditional Religion* (New York: Hutchinson's University Library, 1954), p. 144.

HINDUISM

I. HINDUISM DEFYING DEFINITION

II. HINDUISM BAFFLING DESCRIPTION

III. SOME COMMON CHARACTERISTICS
1. Common Scriptures
2. Common Deities
3. Common Ideals
4. Common Beliefs
5. Common Practices

IV. REFORMED HINDUISM SPEAKING TO US
1. Hindu Reform
2. The Hindu Missionary Thrust
3. The Message of Vedanta

3

Hinduism

THE RELIGION of the masses of India's people is called "Hinduism." The adherents of this religion are called "Hindus." "Hindu" is derived from the word *sindhu*. In the Sanskrit language, it is a term for "river." From this same Sanskrit word came also "Indus," one of the great rivers; "Hindustan," meaning "river-land," and, of course, the word "India" itself. Perhaps 85 per cent of the 400,000,000 or more people of India are Hindus.

I. HINDUISM DEFYING DEFINITION

When one comes to define Hinduism or to answer the question "Who is a Hindu?" he is hard put indeed—even if he is a Hindu! One Hindu scholar states that "Hinduism baffles all attempts to give it an easy and convenient definition."[1] Another has declared that Hinduism cannot be defined because it is "absolutely indefinite." He described it as "all-comprehensive, all-absorbing, all-tolerant, all-complacent, all-compliant." Therefore, a Hindu is a person "who says he is a Hindu, and accepts any of the many beliefs, and follows any of the many practices that are anywhere regarded as Hindu."[2]

Until recently it was common for writers to define Hinduism in terms of caste or the social class into which the individual is born. By this definition, a Hindu is one who belongs to one of the castes and obeys his caste regulations. But even this standard is questioned nowadays at this fluid period in India's social history.

II. Hinduism Baffling Description

If definition seems impossible, so does description. "Hinduism has not been made but has grown. It is a jungle, not a building." [3] It has no creed and no founder. Its origins hark back to the second or third millennium before Christ. Hinduism recognizes no final or absolute truth or revelation. Therefore it absorbs and includes the many expressions of religion in India—if these will permit it—both the primitive belief and practices and those that have developed more recently.

The orthodox Hindu believes in the authority of the ancient scriptures, the Vedas. But, even so, there is still an amazing diversity in the expression of religion. Orthodox Hindus may worship any god or no god. They may attend temple worship regularly or not at all. Their moral code may be strict or loose. "Their only universal obligation, if they are orthodox, is to abide by the rules of their caste and trust that by so doing their next birth will be a happier one." [4]

One can say, therefore, with some humor but also with seriousness, that the three main characteristics of Hinduism are vagueness, variety, and fluidity! [5]

Yet, Hindus insist—and many Western scholars of Hinduism agree—that, for all the baffling diversity of Hinduism, there is an underlying unity of spirit which makes of it one religion.

III. Some Common Characteristics

D. S. Sarma, a famous Hindu teacher, claims that "the soul of Hinduism has ever been the same, even though it has had different embodiments in different ages and among different levels of the people." He says that "There are five elements which contribute to this unity of Hinduism: common scriptures, common deities, common ideals, common beliefs, and common practices." [6]

1. *Common Scriptures*

The most important of the Hindu scriptures are the Vedas and the Epics. The Bhagavata Purana is considered sacred by members of certain sects. The Vedas were written over a period of several centuries, beginning about the eighth century B.C. However, many of them must have existed in oral form since much earlier times. Some may be over four thousand years old!

The word "Veda" means "knowledge," but to the Hindus these Vedas are known as "that which is heard." This phrase indicates something of the reverence accorded the Vedas. They are considered to be eternal, and they form the supreme authority for Hinduism. All other scriptures are secondary and derive their authority from the Vedas.

The Vedas are four in number, the most important being the Rigveda. It is "an anthology of religious poetry in ten books, containing over a thousand hymns and representing the creative efforts of many generations." [7] Each of the four Vedas is divided into four parts, the last of which is the Upanishads, which are profound, philosophic utterances. As the Upanishads come at the end of the Veda, the teaching or philosophy based on them is called "Vedanta," meaning the "end of the Vedas."

The Epics, or heroic poems, are the Mahabharata and the Ramayana. The former includes the Bhagavad Gita, which is said to be "the most important single document in the whole of Hinduism." [8] It was a favorite scripture of the great Gandhi, and he often drew inspiration from it. The romantic stories of these epics are "part of the mother's milk which every Hindu child draws in his infancy." [9]

2. *Common Deities*

The more intellectual of the Hindus tend to believe that Brahma or Brahman (God, or Ultimate Reality) is impersonal. They emphasize the early scriptures which say that "this whole world is Brahma." They also believe that the human soul is the same as Brahma. Therefore, the person has no real individual existence. This doctrine that all things are God is known as pantheism.

The common people are not satisfied with this concept of an impersonal god. They cling to more concrete conceptions and manifestations of deity. Popular imagination centered upon the three great gods: Brahma, the creator; Vishnu, the protector; and Shiva, the destroyer. Other objects of worship are the consorts (wives) of these three.

One of the most widely worshiped deities is Shakti, the consort of Shiva. She is a mother-goddess with various names and forms. One of the characteristic ones is Kali, a four-armed goddess represented as standing on the prostrate form of Shiva. Kali's only clothing is a garland of skulls and a skirt made of the severed hands of demons she has killed. She holds in three of her hands a shield, a sword, and the head of a demon. Her fourth hand is raised in a gesture offering assurance. She is said to represent power which is both gracious and destructive.

Vishnu, the protector, is believed to have come to earth in several forms when world crises required such unusual divine manifestations. Rama, hero of the Ramayana, and Krishna, a character of the Bhagavad Gita, are worshiped as such incarnations of Vishnu.

There are many other gods. These represent diverse cults within the many-storied house of Hinduism. The common man, at least, is encouraged to worship his own favorite deity, while the learned man knows that this is but an accommodation to the average man's need for concreteness. Or the enlightened Hindu worships a god with the knowledge that this deity is but a symbol of the Absolute in one aspect. And he looks beyond the symbol to what he believes is the reality.

Dr. Radhakrishnan, noted Hindu statesman and philosopher, states that there is a graduated scale of worship and knowledge of God in Hinduism. First, in descending order, are the worshipers of the impersonal Absolute; second, those who worship a personal deity; third, the worshipers of God incarnate; fourth, polytheists; and lowest of all, animists, or spirit-worshipers. He admits, however, that the majority of Hindus are satisfied with low places on the scale and that the educated do little to lift them from superstition.[10]

3. Common Ideals

"The cardinal virtues of Hinduism are purity, self-control, detachment, truth, and nonviolence; it is these ideals which have given the people of India a common idea of a good life." [11]

Purity includes both ceremonial and moral aspects. Ceremonial rites of cleansing and prescribed rules concerning food and drink are said to be designed to lead to purity of mind and spirit.

Self-control is aimed both at the flesh and the mind. At the extreme it is asceticism. This is the doctrine that by self-torture or self-denial man can reach high spiritual states. All the great teachers of India have been ascetics, and asceticism is certainly a mark of Hinduism. Yet, "Hinduism at its best does not glorify asceticism," says Professor Sarma. "It does not call upon its followers to suppress the flesh altogether. On the contrary, it teaches that the body is an instrument of righteousness and seeks to regulate its appetites and cravings, teaching the flesh its place." [12]

Detachment is the higher stage of self-control in which one not only overcomes evil but also declares his independence of what is good. For example, one detaches himself from such good things as one's ties to home, family, loved ones, and friends. The Hindu believes that this is renouncing the good in favor of the best. One ceases to cling either to the evil or the good of this life in order to achieve union with the divine Reality.

Truth is this eternal Reality to which life is to be attached. One is instructed by the Hindu scriptures to follow truth wherever it may lead. And truth is usually associated with nonviolence, another of these common ideals of Hinduism. Many Hindus do not agree that nonviolence is necessarily an ideal of Hinduism. However, it cannot be denied that nonviolence has been prominent in Hindu teaching and that Hindu civilization has been relatively peace-loving. Nonviolence applies not only to human beings but also includes kindness to animals, especially the cow.

4. *Common Beliefs*

Beliefs held in common are expressed in modern terms as doctrines of "(a) the evolution of the world; (b) the organization of society; (c) the progress of the individual; (d) the fourfold end of human life; and (e) the law of *karma* and rebirth." [13]

The evolution of the world, according to Hinduism, came about by successive stages, beginning with matter and proceeding through life, consciousness, and intelligence to spiritual perfection. We human beings are at the center of this stage, not seeing the origin of things nor their end. But we do see manifest in the world a graduated scale—from matter to life, to consciousness, to reason, to spiritual perfection.

"A man is nearer to the Supreme Spirit than an animal is; an animal is nearer to Him than a plant, and a plant is nearer to Him than lifeless stone. Similarly, a good man is nearer to the Supreme Spirit than a bad man. . . . The more of such spiritual qualities as goodness, justice, mercy, love and kindness a man has, the nearer he is to the Supreme Being . . . and the more he has of qualities such as cruelty, selfishness, greed, and lust, the nearer he is to the animal." [14]

The belief concerning the organization of society, which is the second of Hinduism's common beliefs, is related to the first. That is, the law of spiritual progression implies a society in which men are ranked according to their spiritual progress or culture. This is attempted in the caste system. This system seems to have its origin in color distinctions between the Caucasian Aryans who early invaded India and the dark-skinned people already inhabiting the land. The word expressing the caste system means "color-duty."

Thus there emerged in quite early times the four main castes: the priestly caste or Brahmans, the warrior class or Kshatriyas, the mercantile and agricultural caste or Vaisyas, and the laboring class or Shudras. In addition, there were the outcastes who were below the Shudras and whose existence was most miserable of all.

This caste system was sanctioned by the scriptures and has been maintained as a divine institution believed to represent the reality of spiritual progression in Hindu society. It was assumed that the most spiritual class was on the top rung of the caste ladder and the least spiritual on the bottom.

The system became exceedingly complex, comprising actually more than three thousand castes. Rules of the caste into which a man was born determined his food, clothing, religious practices, marriage, social contacts, work, and relations to other castes. Conformity to caste regulation was a matter of salvation. One could hope that good behavior in this life, according to caste requirements, would get him promoted to a higher caste in his next life on this earth.

Obviously, this kind of system would provide some order for society. But it could not fail to stifle progress. To the outsider, it appears to be a religious sanction placed upon enforced social inequality. And thoughtful Hindus today recognize that the caste system is doomed because it is entirely contradictory to the conditions of the modern world. So they look for its gradual demise, while holding that its underlying principle of the grading of society according to spiritual progression is valid.

A third unifying belief of Hinduism concerns the spiritual progress of the individual. The ideal is the division of life into four stages. The first is that of the student, in which the youth devotes himself to study and discipline in obedience to a revered teacher. The second stage is that of householder, which involves marriage and the discharge of one's duties to his community and nation. The third step is that of the recluse, who retires from the active life of householder to a secluded place where he can meditate upon spiritual reality. Thus he prepares for the fourth and final stage of holy ascetic (*sannyasin*), who renounces all earthly attachments and gives himself over entirely to communion with the divine.

This is their *ideal* ordering of the life of the individual, and only a small percentage of Hindus practice it. Yet there are many who become *sannyasins* from all castes. The reverence accorded them testifies to the popular belief in the ideal, if not in its practice personally. However, this attitude, too, is being modified in modern India, in favor of a more active life as the ideal of a democratic and progressive nation.

The fourth common belief of Hinduism is the doctrine of the fourfold end of life. This is expressed by four words: *dharma-artha-kama-moksha,* meaning something like "righteousness-material-prosperity-enjoyments-liberation." The larger meaning is that the ultimate goal of man's life is liberation (*moksha*) from bondage to the flesh and the limitations of finite being. However, on the way to this goal man must care for the economic needs of his family (*artha*) and satisfy the animal wants of his body (*kama*). But all this must be done within the limits set by righteousness or moral law (*dharma*).

The fifth doctrine which the Hindus hold in common is the belief in *karma* and *samsara. Karma* is the moral law of cause and effect. It is a most rigid and unyielding form of the principle that whatever a man sows he must reap. The meaning of this law is that what a man is now is the result of what he thought and acted in a past life and that what he is thinking and acting now determines what he shall be in a future life. It assumes that every individual has to pass through a series of lives, either on this earth or elsewhere, before he attains liberation or *moksha*.

This process of birth and rebirth, often called "reincarnation" or "transmigration of souls," is *samsara*. The final goal of life is liberation from this wheel of rebirth, so that one no longer is involved in individual existence but is one with ultimate Reality.

5. *Common Practices*

Every religious Hindu is encouraged to concentrate upon his own chosen deity, worshiping the image of this god every day with flowers and incense. Ideally, at least, he is supposed to be taught to know that this and all deities are but means to realization of the Supreme Spirit.

Worship has almost endless variety. It includes rites in the home and in the temples. It involves sacraments of birth, initiation, marriage, and burial. It includes gifts, offerings, and sacrifices. It is aided by priests, teachers of various ranks and types, and astrologers. It abounds in symbolism and imagery. It concerns itself with fasting, ceremonial bathing, various bodily gestures and postures, dancing, and special clothing and markings of the body. It makes use of prayer beads, repetitions of mystic words, and music. It recognizes the merit of vows and pilgrimages.

Prominent in Hinduism is the practice of *yoga*, a mental discipline for achieving the mystic experience of a vision of or union with the Supreme Spirit. *Yoga* is related to the English word "yoke" and thus means "yoking together" or "union." Its practice is outlined in eight steps, including postures, breath control, and concentration.

In distinction to this specialized meaning, the word *yoga* is used to express three ways of salvation: *karma yoga, bhakti yoga,* and *jnana yoga. Karma yoga* is the way of works or activism or performance of one's religious duties. This is the way followed by the masses. *Bhakti yoga* is the way of devotion, whereby one gives himself in utter loyalty and self-forgetting love to one deity. This, for some Hindus, may be monotheism, and it is not without resemblance to Christian devotion to the one God as revealed in Jesus Christ. This way, too, attracts many. *Jnana yoga* is the way of transcendent divine knowledge which appeals to the philosophically minded. A man may choose his own *yoga,* and all three are considered valid.

Indeed, the whole business of worship is, for the Hindu, an individual matter. Congregational worship is foreign to Hinduism. The aim of worship is individualistic: to realize unity with deity.

Before leaving this subject of religious practices, suppose we look in at a village temple, bearing in mind that worship facilities in the towns and large cities would be more impressive and elaborate.

"Peep into the temple interior; of course, you as a foreigner and therefore an outcaste may not set foot within, or even on the outer threshold. There is a platform in the center, upon which rest certain emblems of the faith, chief of which is the short, smoothly carved pillar of Mahadeva, or the "Great God" Shiva. . . . Along with Shiva on the platform are other symbols: perhaps a rudely carved head of Shiva's consort and an image of the popular Hanuman, the monkey-god, the friend of Rama. Scattered about the platform are flowers, mango leaves, turmeric, grains of rice and wheat, and fragments of coconut—the signs of priestly service. Here and there, especially in niches in the walls, are small clay lamps to be lighted on occasion. From the crossbeam over the doorway hangs a bell. This is the typical shrine of village Hinduism, save for the painted figure of a clock above the doorway! Neither the villager nor the temple ritual is regulated by a clock. Sunrise and sunset bound the rural day, with long repose at midday for man and beast. The priest performs his services mornings and evenings: prayers, gifts, and libations. He serves also on special occasions, in examining horoscopes prior to a marriage; fixing days for plowing, sowing and the harvest; disclosing times when good stars smile on a journey; and conducting the annual ceremony for the dead. His services are indispensable, even as his very presence is a safeguard and a benediction. The women, who have no religious status apart from their husbands, carry on in their houses a daily worship with images from their own god-box. Now and then a villager, or an entire family, goes on a pilgrimage to some distant holy place. Occasionally a *sadhu* (holy man) passes by, feared and frequently revered." [15]

So much, then, for a discussion which may have done justice to the unity of Hinduism but which certainly failed adequately to convey its bewildering diversity.

Now let us ask what Hinduism is saying to the Western world, for as never before it is addressing itself to us.

IV. REFORMED HINDUISM SPEAKING TO US

First of all, we remind ourselves that it is a revived Hinduism which is now speaking to the West—and to its own adherents as well. At the beginning of the nineteenth century, Hinduism, by the admission of present-day Hindus, was stagnant and degraded and steeped in idolatry and superstition. Then came the flood of Western influences which inundated India—and most of the East—during the modern period. One result was that reform was provoked within Hinduism, especially by the Christian influences from the West.

1. *Hindu Reform*

Reform took two directions, illustrated by the two most prominent early reform movements. The Brahmo Samaj was founded in 1828 by Ram Mohun Roy, a very able, sincere man of fine education. He was well acquainted with Islam, Buddhism, and Christianity, as well as his native Hinduism. Repelled by the polytheistic, idolatrous, superstitious religion of his day which sanctioned atrocious social and moral abuses, he founded his own cult or sect within Hinduism. Insofar as he drew upon Hindu sources, he looked to the later Vedas, called the Upanishads.

The religion of the Brahmo Samaj was liberal and contained elements from various religions. But it insisted on spiritual worship of the one God. Its prominent characteristic was vigorous social reform. It set itself resolutely against such abuses as child marriage, the cremation of the widow on her husband's funeral pyre, and caste. In spite of the smallness of the movement and the schisms which it has suffered, the Brahmo Samaj has been quite influential. One branch of it moved quite close to Christianity.

In contrast to the liberalism of the Brahmo Samaj were "orthodox" movements. One of the most prominent was the Arya Samaj, founded in 1875 by Dayananda Sarisvati. This was a "back to the Vedas" movement, taking its stand on these authoritative scriptures. Unlike the Brahmo Samaj, which tried to adjust Hinduism to the modern situation, the Arya Samaj sought to rejuvenate India by a return to original Hinduism. It opposes idol worship and the caste system and advocates social reform and monotheism. Strongly nationalistic, it tends to be more political than religious. It seeks to make new converts and to reconvert those who have forsaken Hinduism. It is an adamant enemy of Christianity and of all who make inroads on Hindu religion.

The reform movements, of which these were significant

examples, combined with the remarkable influence of individual reformers. These reforms stood within the Hindu tradition. Nevertheless, they drank deeply from other fountains of Western culture and Christian religion. Rabindranath Tagore wrote mystical poetry with a universal appeal. He also traveled widely throughout the world in the interest of international peace, speaking out against national exploitation and aggression. Mahatma Gandhi attained the stature of world sainthood and continues to affect the world tremendously by his doctrine and practice of nonviolent resistance. While profoundly influenced by Christianity and strongly attracted by the person of Jesus, Gandhi remained a loyal Hindu.

Both Tagore and Gandhi are dead, but Vinoba Bhave continues in their train, representing Hinduism at its best, as did they. This strange, selfless man walks barefooted throughout India, effecting social reform by persuading large landholders to divide their land with the poor. And there are others like these three.

2. *The Hindu Missionary Thrust*

Thus Hinduism has been prepared for a new thrust into the Western world with a message refined and adjusted to the modern situtation. This message is Vedanta and its most outstanding medium of communication is the Ramakrishna Mission.

The Ramakrishna movement consists of both the Ramakrishna Math (or monastic order) and the Ramakrishna Mission. It was founded by and received its name from Ramakrishna Paramahamsa (1836–1886), a most remarkable Indian holy man.

A poor priest with little education, Ramakrishna became "god-intoxicated" through intense worship of the mysterious and fierce-appearing goddess Kali, who was for him the Divine Mother of the universe. He tried the way of other

Hindu cults and of Islam and Christianity, in each case experiencing what he understood as union with their deities. The result was a conviction of the harmony of all religions which he expressed thus: "Different creeds are but different paths to reach the one God."

Ramakrishna gathered about him disciples, one of whom organized the movement as a missionary invasion of the Western world. This was the brilliant, learned, and eloquent man who is known internationally as Swami Vivekananda (1863-1900). The Ramakrishna movement was introduced to the West through Vivekananda's electrifying address at the Parliament of Religions held in connection with the World's Fair in Chicago in 1893. He continued to captivate audiences and make converts in the three years that he remained in North America and Europe. Before he left the United States he placed his work on a permanent basis by establishing the Vedanta Society of New York and providing for it a leadership.

In 1957 the Math and Mission was reported to have 138 centers, 52 of which were distributed in ten countries outside India, including one each in France, England, and Argentina, and eleven in the United States. There is a varied program of religious and cultural work, conducting of schools, medical treatment and nursing, and relief work. The centers in this country are designed for the first of these categories, religious and cultural work. This includes propagating the message of "the spiritual unity of mankind" by lectures and by the publication and distribution of literature.

3. The Message of Vedanta

What is the message of Vedanta which these centers propagate? Vedanta is a profound Hindu philosophy which as such is not easily described briefly. As preached by the "guest teachers" of the Ramakrishna Mission, however, it may be summarized as follows:

(1) Ultimate Reality, that which alone has real existence, is pure Spirit, pure Being. (2) The physical universe is an appearance which disappears when full knowledge of the Real is attained. (3) Ultimate Reality, the Supreme Being, is the creator, preserver, and absorber of the universe and is manifest in the physical world as the one all-pervasive Self. (4) Man is essentially divine. That is, the inner self of man is identical with the one world Self. (5) To realize this essential divinity is the supreme end of man's life. (6) Methods of this realization vary according to the different tendencies, capacities, and situations of those so aspiring. (7) The different religions are but different ways leading ultimately to the Divine. (8) Therefore, attempts to convert members of one religion to another are expressions of intolerance and bigotry.

This message makes an appeal to the people of America because of its emphasis on the spiritual, which challenges materialism, and particularly because of its seeming broadmindedness and large tolerance. Although a few famous people of America and Europe have been converted to it, it insists quite sincerely that it desires to make no converts to a Vedanta or Ramakrishna cult or organization.

The subtle fallacy is that a Christian cannot accept this message as truth without being converted from his faith that God has uniquely revealed himself in Jesus Christ. The Christian cannot think of God as an impersonal Absolute whose divinity is to be equated with man's. He knows him as the holy, living, personal God who bridges the gap between himself and fallen humanity only by a stable, a cross, and an empty tomb.

No doubt many churchgoing Americans who have never heard of Vedanta are more Vedantist than Christian in theology. They believe that one religion is as good as another, since all have the same goal. But this is an essential tenet of Vedanta, not Christianity.

D. T. Niles is a famous world Christian leader from Ceylon whose ancestors are Indians and Hindus. On a visit to our country, Dr. Niles remarked that he "had never seen a purer version of Vedanta than the present popular version of religion in America!" [16] To this we shall return in the final chapter.

FOR CLASS DISCUSSION

1. Is there real unity in Hinduism? Discuss.
2. What are the common beliefs of Hinduism?
3. What is wrong with the doctrine of *karma*, the law of cause and effect in Hinduism?
4. What is the main difference between Vedanta and Christianity?

NOTES

[1] Swami Nikhilananda, *Hinduism: Its Meaning for the Liberation of the Spirit* (New York: Harper and Brothers, 1958), p. 3. Used by permission of Harper and Row, Publishers, Inc.

[2] Quoted in Soper, *The Religions of Mankind,* pp. 102–103. Used by permission of Abingdon Press.

[3] Sir Charles Eliot, quoted in A. C. Bouquet, *Hinduism* (New York: Hutchinson's University Library, 1948), p. 13. Used by permission of Hillary House Publishers, Ltd.

[4] Noss, *Man's Religions,* pp. 113–114. Used by permission of The Macmillan Company.

[5] Bouquet, *op. cit.*, pp. 11–12.

[6] D. S. Sarma, "The Nature and History of Hinduism," *The Religion of the Hindus,* ed. Kenneth W. Morgan (New York: The Ronald Press Company, 1953), p. 7. Used by permission of The Ronald Press Company.

[7] Noss, *op. cit.*, p. 117.

[8] Bouquet, *op. cit.*, p. 82.

[9] Sarma, *op. cit.*, p. 8.

[10] S. Radhakrishnan, *The Hindu View of Life* (New York: The Macmillan Company, 1927), pp. 32–33. Used with permission of The Macmillan Company.

[11] Sarma, *op. cit.*, p. 12.

[12] *Ibid.*

[13] Sarma, *op. cit.*, p. 13.

[14] *Ibid.*, p. 14.

[15] *Faiths Men Live By*, Second Edition, by John Clark Archer and Carl E. Purinton. Copyright 1958, The Ronald Press Company.

[16] Edmund Perry, *The Gospel in Dispute* (Garden City: Doubleday and Company, 1958), p. 15. Copyright 1958 by Edmund Perry. Reprinted by permission of Doubleday and Company, Inc.

BUDDHISM

4

Buddhism

LIKE HINDUISM, Buddhism is a product of the fertile religious soil of India. Indeed, it is best understood as a reform movement within Hinduism. It was a protest against the ritualism, polytheism, and caste distinctions of early Hinduism. It also rejected the early philosophical development of Hinduism and turned to psychology and a way of self-salvation.

I. THE ORIGIN OF BUDDHISM

Buddhism had its origin in the life, teaching, and personality of an extraordinary Indian sage, Siddhartha Gautama, the son of a ruler of the Sakya clan in northern India. The life span of Gautama is usually reckoned as about 560–480 B.C. Gautama is often called by the title "Buddha," meaning the "Enlightened One."

Legend and myth have accumulated about the birth and life of the Buddha. For instance, one of the birth legends has him standing and walking immediately after birth and roaring out in a lordly voice, "I am the chief in the world!"

Since the Indian mind had little concern for history, it is difficult to separate the facts about Gautama from these legends. But traditional accounts indicate that throughout his boyhood and youth, Gautama enjoyed the luxurious and sensuous life of his father's court. He was carefully shielded from the tragic realities of human existence.

When Gautama was twenty-nine, the gods then took the initiative and showed him the "Four Passing Sights." Thus he saw in succession a frail and decrepit old man, a loathsome corpse, a person with a repulsive disease, and a calm and peaceful recluse. Gautama was shocked by this revelation, and filled with a desire to find deliverance from the misery of existence. He forsook his life of luxury, left his beautiful and devoted wife and his newborn son, and took the life of a recluse.

Then ensued six years of quest and striving in which Gautama carefully considered ways of salvation suggested by teachers. Finally he gave himself over to the strictest self-denial, to the extent that he almost perished. In the ancient scriptures, his fasting is described in the most vivid terms. Gautama himself is represented as saying: "When I thought I would touch the skin of my stomach, I actually took hold of my spine . . . so much did the skin of my stomach cling to my spine through the little food." [1]

Perceiving the folly of this extreme method, he began to eat again and to try another way. Shortly thereafter, while seated in meditation under a tree, he attained the enlightenment which Buddhists call omniscience, or perfect knowledge. Thus he became a Buddha.

After a period of temptation, Gautama made the great decision to preach. He would share his experience with others that they, too, might enter the bliss of enlightenment. By his preaching he won converts, and soon a brotherhood of monks was formed, with Gautama at the head. His ministry continued for about forty-five years, until his death at the age of eighty. He died of indigestion, according to the early scriptures. With characteristic thoughtfulness he sent word to his host who had fed him, thanking him for helping him to the final stage of *Nirvana!*

The preaching of Gautama and the founding of his order of monks represent the beginning of a new religion. The monks were initiated with the confession of the Three Refuges: "I take refuge in the Buddha. I take refuge in the Dharma (his doctrine). I take refuge in the Sangha (the order of his disciples)." Monks also took vows to obey the Ten Precepts:

1. Refrain from destroying life.
2. Do not take what is not given.
3. Abstain from unchastity.
4. Do not lie or deceive.
5. Abstain from intoxicants.
6. Eat moderately and not after noon.
7. Do not look at dancing, singing, or dramatic spectacles.
8. Do not affect the use of garlands, scents, unguents, or ornaments.
9. Do not use high or broad beds.
10. Do not accept gold or silver.[2]

Laymen were admitted to the Order, continuing in their secular occupations. They were required to obey the first five of the Ten Precepts and to promote the progress of the Order. These numerous lay associates gave great strength to the movement. Women also were finally admitted and an order of nuns was formed, though Buddha was very reluctant to give permission.

II. BUDDHISM'S BASIC IDEAS

What are the essential doctrines which the Buddha taught? About some of his teaching there is considerable uncertainty. However, the pure Orthodox Buddhists' interpretation of Gautama's essential doctrines seems fairly clear. He retained from Hinduism the concepts of *samsara*, the endless cycle of rebirths, and *karma*, the law of cause and effect—though his idea of liberation gave more flexibility to *karma*. Buddha's enlightenment brought him the insight that all things are impermanent, always in a state of constant flux; substanceless, having neither permanent self nor soul; and involved in suffering. Man in his ignorance attaches himself to the impermanent and substanceless and thus becomes subject to misery and suffering.

Early Buddhist scriptures indicate that the Buddha constructed a thought-ladder termed "Dependent Origination." This was designed to show that the "entire mass of suffering —old age, death, sorrow, lamentation, pain, grief, and despair" —is rooted finally in ignorance. Upon the obliteration of ignorance, through enlightenment, this whole chain of seeming reality disappears and "thus, the entire mass of suffering ceases." [3]

Gautama's experience of enlightenment is set forth more simply in the sermon which he is reported to have preached to his five first converts in the Deer Park at Benares. Proclaiming the "Middle Path" which lay between the two extremes of self-indulgence and self-mortification, he declared the "Four Noble Truths": (1) Suffering is a universal fact. (2) The origin of suffering is in craving or desire. (3) The cessation of suffering is accomplished by the forsaking of desire. (4) The way leading to the end of desire and the cessation of suffering is the Noble Eightfold Path of right view, right-mindedness, right speech, right action, right livelihood, right effort, right-mindfulness, and right concentration.

The consequence of following the Eightfold Path is *Nirvana,* the state in which desire is extinguished. Buddhists insist that *Nirvana* is not the negative experience of "nothingness" or "annihilation," but the positive experience of "freedom" or "emancipation."

A monk may reach the experience of enlightenment and entrance into *Nirvana* in this life. Such a one is called an *arahat.* For him all craving is gone. He knows the impermanence of the self, so there is nothing about him to be born again, to live again, or to die again. Full *Nirvana* comes to him at death when the constituents of the Self are finally dispersed.

This concept of *Nirvana* suggests two things: First, the desire to cling to individual existence as a person must be extinguished. Second, there is an impersonal Reality into which one can be absorbed.

The layman cannot hope to reach *Nirvana* in this life, but he can amass merit for a next existence which will be more favorable for attaining the ultimate goal. In addition to living according to the first five vows, mentioned on page 47, he is expected to perform ministries of service to his family and community and to the monks.

Buddhist writings attribute everything about a person to what he has done and thought in previous existences. *Karma* (the law of cause and effect) determines longevity, health, physical appearance, wealth, social status, and intelligence. But the Buddha taught that through following the Noble Eightfold Path one could break the chain of rebirths and thus overcome the accumulation of bad *karma*. This salvation was possible for people of all castes.

Here, then, is an impressive way of self-salvation, acknowledging and relying upon no god whatsoever.

What has been said thus far is descriptive of original or early Buddhism and of Theravada or southern Buddhism which has tried to maintain the religion essentially unchanged. Look now at the major divisions of Buddhism and how they differ.

III. DIVISION AND EXPANSION

Buddhism developed considerable strength in India, especially under King Asoka, who was an ardent Buddhist of the third century B.C. He sent missionaries of this religion to other countries. The most notable result was the conversion of Ceylon to Buddhism. A few centuries later, for reasons not entirely clear, this faith died out in India, and Ceylon became the stronghold of original Buddhism.

In the meantime, differences began to develop between southern and northern Buddhism, resulting in two major divisions. Northern Buddhists called their religion "Maha-yana," meaning "Great Vehicle," and southern Buddhism, "Hinayana," or "Little Vehicle." Understandably, this name was displeasing to southern Buddhists who prefer the desig-nation "Theravada," meaning "Way of the Elders."

Through early missionary expansion, Buddhism has been planted widely throughout Asia. Theravada predominates in Ceylon, Burma, Thailand, Cambodia, and Laos; Mahayana is found principally in China, Tibet, and Japan, and to lesser extent in Korea and Viet Nam.

Statistics for world Buddhist membership vary widely. A figure of about 300,000,000 is frequently given, but estimates range all the way from 100,000,000 to 500,000,000. A recent Buddhist writer has indicated 150,000,000 as "the figure which has fairly wide acceptance."[4] At any rate, both as to numerical strength and total influence, Buddhism in both its branches is a significant factor in the modern world.

IV. THERAVADA AND MAHAYANA

1. *Agreements*

The two divisions of Buddhism, Theravada and Mahayana, have a great deal in common. They share the beliefs in *karma*, dependent origination, and transmigration of souls, though with differences of interpretation. They agree that the en-lightenment of *Nirvana* is the final human goal, that *Nirvana* is attained by following the right path (though not an identi-cal path for all sects), and that this blissful goal is ultimately possible for all people. The two concur in holding in rever-ence the "Three Jewels," namely, the Buddha, the Doctrine, and the Order. Both groups have maintained the lofty ideal of compassion or mercy for all living beings.

They share with Hinduism the emphasis upon the primacy of spiritual values. Like Hinduism, also, both branches of Buddhism take pride in tolerance. That this tolerance has allowed the incorporation into Buddhism of much that is superstitious and polytheistic is recognized by Buddhist scholars.

On the international scene, Theravada and Mahayana have reached some measure of union in the recently organized World Fellowship of Buddhists.

All these indications of agreement, however, should not obscure the fact that between these two major branches of Buddhism there are differences profound enough to make them look like two different religions.

2. *Differences*

A fundamental difference is that of spirit or attitude. Theravada is conservative, holding tenaciously to Gautama's supposed atheism and his reliance upon self-salvation. Mahayana, on the other hand, is less conservative and more "religious" in spirit. It attempts to make replies to questions left unanswered by original Buddhism and to accommodate itself to the deep religious hungers of mankind. It has been significantly modified by its centuries of association with the other religions of East Asia, especially Chinese and Japanese religions, with which it has tended to blend.

Basic, also, to the variance between Theravada and Mahayana are their differing scriptures. Theravada accepts the Pali language scriptures of early Buddhism and rejects the later scriptures. The Mahayana canon includes the Pali scriptures, translated into Sanskrit and other Asiatic languages; but Mahayanists have accepted into their canon other scriptures which they deem more important. Moreover, the various Mahayana sects emphasize their own favorite scriptures to the relative neglect of others.

Another point of difference concerns the several Buddhas mentioned in the Pali scriptures. Theravada pays almost exclusive devotion to Gautama. Mahayana emphasizes the eternal Buddha Reality rather than its historical manifestation in Gautama. Furthermore, some Mahayana sects pay more attention to other Buddhas than Gautama as expressions of the eternal Buddha.

Conflicting interpretations of Gautama's own person and ministry have resulted in two different ideals of the Buddhist life. The Theravada ideal is the *arahat*, the monk who, wandering like the lone rhinoceros, makes his way straight toward the goal of *Nirvana*. The Mahayana ideal is the *bodhisattva*, one who delays the full enjoyment of *Nirvana* for the sake of serving others.

Closely related to this difference in ideal is the tendency for Mahayana to give greater stress than does Theravada to social service. In Theravada, the motive for charity and acts of compassion seems to be the desire to produce good *karma* and to express one's identity with all that lives. It is especially meritorious to serve the monks of the Order. In Mahayana, compassion seems more definitely based upon the sacrificial example of Gautama and other Buddhas to lead others to *Nirvana* rather than selfishly to enjoy it—based upon the *bodhisattva* ideal.

V. The Buddhist at Worship

1. *The Trappings of Religion*

Buddhism has its share of the trappings of religion: images, relics, temples, offerings, rituals, monasteries, priests, pilgrimages, and the like. This is true even of Theravada which insists that there is no god, that prayer and ceremony have no value, and that man's only hope for salvation lies in himself.

Especially interesting is the pagoda, the most characteristic feature of Buddhist architecture. The pagoda is a many-storied tower, varying in appearance in different world areas. The pagodas of Burma, for example, have a tall, serpentine effect, while those of China and Japan have an ascending series of gracefully curved roofs. Pagodas are usually connected with a temple and are often supposed to house a relic of the Buddha.

There are countless images of Buddha. They are in sitting, standing, or reclining postures and usually reflecting the calm and peace of his enlightenment. In size, they range all the way from the tiny images which may be found in homes or offered in worship, to the giant statues such as the *Dai-butsu* ("Great Buddha") in Kamakura, Japan. This image of the Buddha seated in contemplation is fifty feet in height and thirty-six feet from knee to knee!

2. *Worship in Theravada Buddhism*

The Shwedagon Temple of Theravada Buddhism in Rangoon, Burma, is the largest and finest one in Southeast Asia. The temple is a most impressive sight, with its gilded pagoda towering above the city and dominating the entire landscape. It is profusely gilded from base to summit and ornamented with jeweled bells hanging from the umbrella-like top. It is surrounded by four chapels and numerous *stupas* or shrines donated and erected by faithful laymen. Also on the top level are one of the largest wooden bells in the world and a colossal reclining statue of the Buddha.

Here one may see Theravada Buddhist worshipers from all over Southeast Asia, but especially from Burma. They pause for worship at the chapels and *stupas*, bowing in meditation before the Buddha images and leaving gifts on the altars.

"Among the worshipers the monk is most conspicuous. . . . With his shaven head, in his own peculiar garb, fingering his rosary, his lips moving without sound, he seems cut off from the world of matter, cherishing only deep religious thoughts. . . . He prostrates himself with dignity before an alabaster Buddha-image set with sparkling jewels. This attracts the laymen as they pass. They pause and seat themselves on the floor, ready to follow him as he prays. . . . He has no god. The

Buddha is merely the pattern of what he, too, would become. As the monk prays, his 'prayer' is merely meditation on the 'truths' the Buddha taught. . . . He seeks deliverance, but his hope lies in himself and his code.

"But the people in the temple? What of them? They, also, look upon the image, and they pray. They may, perhaps naively, be idolaters. To many of them the Buddha doubtless is of heavenly essence and a god. Most of them fix their thoughts on him as God. . . . Indeed, the monk himself may be an object of devotion. He is, at least, a good example. Once they may have known him as an ordinary man; now he has severed his 'attachments,' and they revere him. Then, beyond him, is his own pattern, the Buddha, whom they may see in him. We may call their reverence worship, especially if it be directed to the Buddha. Such is the quality of their prayers, prostrations, flower-offerings, and lighted candles. They do not always worship with the monks; they engage in their devotions when and where they will." [5]

3. *Mahayana Worship*

Worship for the Mahayanist is quite dissimilar, partly because it is much more complex. There is a highly organized hierarchy with various ranks, often including married priests as well as celibate monks. Temple worship includes ceremonies of various sorts: morning devotions, vespers, masses for the dead, funerals, and various memorial services. Altars are often extremely elaborate and of the finest artistic design. Images are of great variety, because the saints and divine personages of Mahayana which they depict are very numerous. Mahayana has provided the common man with heavens and hells and savior-gods. It has exchanged the nonphilosophical religion of original Buddhism for profound philosophical systems.

The philosophically minded monk of Mahayana Buddhism may know that behind all the ceremonies of his religion stands only absorption into *Nirvana* as the ultimate. The common man is usually satisfied with belief in a savior and promise of a blissful life in heaven. The most popular sects of Mahayana are the "Pure Land" sects that promise a heavenly salvation for those who put simple trust in the Buddha called *Amitabha*. So there is no doubt about the prayers of the common man here: They are real petitions addressed to a savior-god.

Neither in Mahayana nor Theravada is worship congregational, even if led by groups of monks. As in Hinduism, it is an individual matter, though it does not overlook family rites.

"In all Buddhist lands the devout laymen have shrines in their homes where they perform their individual devotions morning and evening. Such shrines are decorated with images, offerings of flowers, water, incense, and lamps, sometimes with cooked foods, vegetables, and fruits, depending upon the customs of the country. In Japan tablets bearing the religious names of the ancestors are placed beside the image of the Buddha on the family shrine." [6]

VI. THE MISSIONARY REVIVAL OF BUDDHISM

It has been pointed out that Buddhism's present extent in Asia is due to its missionary expansion, especially in its early history. The Buddhist scriptures record a kind of "Great Commission" issued by the Buddha. "Go forth, O monks," he said, "for the good of the many, for the happiness of the many, out of compassion for the world."

However, Buddhism never seems seriously to have contemplated a truly universal mission until very recently. It is now a "self-consciously missionary faith." [7] Its sense of mission, at least in part, is motivated by a desire to counteract the effects of the Christian mission. Buddhists declare that Buddhism, and not Christianity, is the religion offering the best hope of world peace. The alleged aggressive, exclusive, and domineering spirit of Christianity is contrasted with the peaceful, tolerant, and broad-minded religion of the gentle Buddha.

"Buddhist monks and Burmese students, as well as Buddhists in other nations of Asia, are calling to their religious fellows to support a world mission of Buddhism—'to save the world from Christianity, which has failed to prevent the so-called Christian nations of the West from involving mankind in two world wars, with the threat of a third and even more disastrous one.'" [8]

Buddhism is paralleling developments in the Christian ecumenical movement by the founding of a World Fellowship of Buddhists. This organization held several great Buddhist World Congresses in the 1950's, climaxed in 1956 by the celebration of the 2500th anniversary of the death of Buddha. Thus there have been brought into union, or at least into vital fellowship, the two great branches of Buddhism, which possibly differ from each other more basically than Protestantism and Roman Catholicism. The motivation for this union seems to be the new awareness of a Buddhist world mission.

The missionary movement of Buddhism is itself largely unorganized, but it has the support of powerful agencies. They include the Maha Bodhi Society for Theravada Buddhism and the Young East Association for Mahayana, as well as the World Fellowship just mentioned. In addition, it has the sympathy of most Asian governments and the active support of some. For example, the Buddhists of Burma, under the inspiration and sponsorship of Premier Thakin Nu, have constructed in Rangoon a World Peace Pagoda and a Missionary Training College. Here Buddhist monks may spend five years in training, including language study for missionary work in the Western countries and in India, where Buddhism is once more growing. [9]

In Ceylon, advertisements are displayed, inviting subscriptions to a missionary society "for the spread of the Gospel of Buddhism among the heathen of Europe." Shinshu, the strongest sect of Japanese Buddhism, by the mid-1950's was maintaining 130 missionaries on the American continent. Careful plans are laid to introduce Buddhism into so-called Christian countries where there is now disillusionment with Christianity, especially among intellectuals. [10]

It is claimed, also, that many of the young intellectuals of America—the "beat generation"—are being converted to Zen Buddhism. This is said to be a reaping of the harvest planted by over fifty years of Hindu and Buddhist missionary efforts in the metropolitan areas of America. Zen study centers have been added to the Ramakrishna centers and other societies of Eastern religions in most of our large cities. [11]

Though in this aspect Zen may be little more than a fad in America, it is still true that some Westerners have been converted to a serious espousal of this religion. One of them, Mr. Christmas Humphreys, founded the Buddhist Society in London in 1924 as a center from which information about Zen could be disseminated.

Therefore, some brief word is in order about Zen as the sect most influential in the West.

VII. ZEN AND THE WEST

Zen Buddhism is a Japanese denomination, imported to Japan from China several centuries ago. It has some nine or ten million followers in Japan, but its influence upon Japanese culture is far out of proportion to its numerical strength.

Zen is almost impossible of definition, because it shuns the expression of truth in ideas or concepts. It insists that truth can only be known intuitively. Truth must be experienced or realized through the awakening of intuitive wisdom by means of meditation. This meditation is best accomplished under the direction of a Zen master who helps bring his pupil to enlightenment. Correct postures and set times of meditation are practiced. Sharp exchanges of questions and answers, suddenly shouted words and paradoxical sayings are used to help awaken insight.

For example, if a monk asks a master, "What is Zen?" he may meet with the reply, "Zen is a broken piece of brick." Or if he asks, "Who is the Buddha?" he may be told, "The cat climbs the post." Then, if he expresses perplexity, he may be directed to ask the post!

Such methods are designed to bring logic to a standstill and throw one back on intuition, with the possibility that a sudden flash of insight will bring him to a direct experience of reality. Though these methods often manifest a quaint humor, it should not be concluded that Zen is easy or lacking in seriousness. Those who make of it a fad or cult in America might be surprised to hear of the experience of a Zen convert. Mrs. Ruth Fuller Sasaki is a Chicago native who converted to Zen and is now a Zen priestess directing a temple in Kyoto, Japan. In learning Zen, Mrs. Sasaki had to accustom herself to days at a time with one hour's sleep per night and eighteen hours of meditation without a break! It often takes more than ten years of strenuous discipline for a Zen monk even to begin to experience enlightenment.

If Zen is to be expressed in terms of doctrine, a Zennist should be permitted to express it. This is the way Mrs. Sasaki puts it:

". . . Zen holds that there is no god outside the universe who has created it and created man. God—if I may borrow that word for a moment—the universe, and man are one indissoluble existence, one total whole. Only THIS—capital THIS—is. Anything and everything that appears to us as an individual entity or phenomenon, whether it be a planet or an atom, a mouse or a man, is but a temporary manifestation of THIS in form; every activity that takes place, whether it be birth or death, loving or eating breakfast, is but a temporary manifestation of THIS in activity. When we look at things this way, naturally we cannot believe that each individual person has been endowed with a special and individual soul or self. Each of us is but a cell as it were, in the body of the Great Self, a cell that comes into being, performs its functions, and passes away, transformed into another manifestation. Though we have temporary individuality, that temporary, limited individuality is not either a true self or our true self. Our true self is the Great Self. . . ." [12]

Why does Zen appeal to the West? No doubt an intuitive, subjective approach to religion appeals to an age which has emphasized human reason and scientific objectivity. Perhaps Zen appeals because it is a flight from dogma and doctrine. Maybe it is the pull of a religion that promises peace and tranquility without well-defined morality. Undoubtedly the motive of nonconformity in a conformist culture is at work here. Also, there is the attractiveness of a religion of tolerance which makes Zen, along with Vedanta, seem appropriate to modern man's refusal of absolute standards of truth.

Besides this, there may be a Western guilt complex for the sins of Western domination of the Eastern world. So there is a tendency to accept everything Eastern as naturally superior to what the West has to offer. Add to these factors the postwar contacts of Americans with Japan and Japanese culture and the appeal of Zen arts to the West. Zen also has some resemblance to existentialism, a thought movement popular in Europe. Then, too, there are the writings of the great interpreter and exponent of Zen, D. T. Suzuki, and the testimonies of Zen converts such as Christmas Humphreys and Mrs. Sasaki.

Thus, there are many possible and probable factors in explaining the relative popularity of Zen in our culture. Read the writing of Westerners who have adopted Zen, however, and you will almost invariably discover another element: there is obvious relief in getting rid of the idea of God as an independent sovereign, personal Will with whom man must reckon. As one of them has expressed it:

"The appeal of Zen, as of other forms of Eastern philosophy, is that it unveils behind the urgent realm of good and evil a vast region of oneself about which there need be no guilt or recrimination, where at last the self is indistinguishable from God.

"But the Westerner who is attracted by Zen and who would understand it deeply must have one indispensable qualification: he must understand his own culture so thoroughly that he is no longer swayed by its premises unconsciously. He must really have come to terms with the Lord God Jehovah and with his Hebrew-Christian conscience so that he can take it or leave it without fear or rebellion." [13]

So the holy God of the Bible, the God and Father of our Lord Jesus Christ, must first be reduced to something one can take or leave. Then one comes to rest in the "vast region . . . where at last the self is indistinguishable from God."

Therefore, is not the real appeal of Zen the modern—but ancient—flight from God through enlightenment? Is there not a hint of a story of a garden and a tree of knowledge, and a beguiling serpent who assures the human inhabitants that, in spite of the limits set by their Creator, they might eat of that tree? "When you eat of it," he told them, "your eyes will be opened, and you will be like God" (Gen. 3:5, RSV).

FOR CLASS DISCUSSION

1. Compare the life of Gautama with the life of Jesus.
2. What are the main beliefs of Buddhism?
3. Is Buddhism a missionary faith? Why?
4. What is Zen? Why does it appeal to some people in America and Europe?

NOTES

[1] Quoted in Edward J. Thomas, *The Life of Buddha as Legend and History*, third edition, revised (London: Routledge and Kegan Paul, Ltd., 1949), p. 65. Used by permission of Routledge and Kegan Paul, Ltd.

[2] Buddhist Scriptures, quoted in Noss, *Man's Religions*, p. 164. Used by permission of The Macmillan Company.

[3] J. Kashyap, "Origin and Expansion of Buddhism," *The Path of the Buddha*—Buddhism Interpreted by Buddhists, ed. Kenneth W. Morgan (New York: The Ronald Press Company, 1956), pp. 25–26. Used by permission of The Ronald Press Company.

[4] Hajime Nakamura, "Unity and Diversity in Buddhism," *The Path of the Buddha*, ed. Morgan, p. 364.

[5] Archer, *op. cit.*, pp. 259–261.

[6] Nakamura, *op. cit.*, p. 397.

[7] Rajah B. Manikam, ed., *Christianity and the Asian Revolution* (New York: Friendship Press, 1954), p. 141. Used by permission of Friendship Press.

[8] George Appleton, *The Christian Approach to the Buddhist* (London: Edinburgh House Press, 1958), p. 49.

[9] Manikam, *op. cit.*, pp. 140–141; Perry, *op. cit.*, pp. 20–21.

[10] *Ibid.*

[11] Peter Fingesten, "Beat and Buddhist," *The Christian Century*, February 25, 1959, p. 226.

[12] Ruth Fuller Sasaki, "Zen: A Method for Religious Awakening," *The World of Zen: An East-West Anthology*, ed., Nancy Wilson Ross (New York: Random House, 1960), p. 18. Used by permission of Ruth F. Sasaki. Published separately in booklet form by The First Zen Institute of America, 113 East 30th Street, New York, N.Y.

[13] Alan Watts, "Beat Zen, Square Zen, and Zen," *The World of Zen: An East-West Anthology*, p. 334. Used by permission of City Lights Books.

CHINESE RELIGIONS

I. THE GENERAL CHARACTERISTICS OF CHINESE RELIGIONS
   1. Basic Attitudes
   2. Fundamental Concepts

II. TAOISM
   1. The Founder
   2. The Tao Te Ching
   3. Taoist Religion

III. CONFUCIANISM
   1. The Life of Confucius
   2. The Teaching of Confucius
   3. The Development of Confucianism

IV. POPULAR RELIGION

V. THE PRESENT SITUATION

5

Chinese Religions

CHINA IS the birthplace of two of the world's religions, Confucianism and Taoism. Confucianism is more influential as an ethical system than as a religious cult. Taoism has tended, on the one hand, to become a philosophy or, on the other hand, to revert to magic and primitive religion. As a religion, Buddhism is more prominent in China than either of these, but, of course, it is not native to China.

I. THE GENERAL CHARACTERISTICS OF CHINESE RELIGIONS

1. *Basic Attitudes*

The central belief of the ancient Chinese is that heaven, earth, and man are so closely related that what happens to one affects the others. If man misbehaves, or even the emperor alone, all of nature is upset, as well as heaven. When man behaves correctly, there is universal harmony. "The crops will thrive and men will be at peace and prosperous." [1]

A second basic attitude is tolerance toward other religious ideas. This open-minded attitude permits a man to be simultaneously a Confucianist, Taoist, and Buddhist. Or, at different times or in different aspects of his life he may be all of these. This attitude is akin to, but not identical with, the spirit of India which tends to absorb everything into the one religion, Hinduism.

A third and closely related attitude is a practical and ethical emphasis in Chinese religions. "The essential purpose and function of religion is not to try to know the unknowable or explain the inexplicable, not to trace the origin of the universe and explore the mysteries of life; but to formulate rules and to set down principles for dealing with life as it is, in order to make it richer and nobler. Religion is for life, and not life for religion." [2]

2. *Fundamental Concepts*

In Chinese religious thought, the concept of heaven is basic. Heaven has nothing to do with the after-life, as Christians think of the term. Rather, heaven is the sky thought of as a deity. The overarching heaven is considered to be the first great object of worship in China.

The ancient Chinese were impressed by the order and harmony of the celestial regions. Harmony and well-being on earth could be maintained only by obedience to the well-ordered rule of heaven.

A second fundamental idea of Chinese religions is the Tao. Literally, Tao means a "way" or "road." The universe operates in a certain "way" or follows a definite "path" or pattern. Thus the Tao is the eternal preordained "way-to-go." It is the harmonizing principle of the universe. It is a universal law or law of life. So there is the myth of a "golden age" when the emperors led the people in perfect conformity to the Tao. The Tao itself is impersonal and the deities are its mediators.

The third basic concept may be older than the Tao—or again, it may be a further development and amplification of it. This is the concept of the *yang* and the *yin*. From the interaction of these two dynamic principles, life and matter are produced. These principles are responsible also for the variety and change of the universe.

The *yang* is the masculine or heavenly principle: aggressive, positive, bright, warm, dry, and procreative. The *yin* is the female or earthy principle: passive, negative, dark, cold, wet, secretive, fertile. Objects manifest these two, though either *yang* or *yin* may completely dominate. For example, the sun is almost entirely *yang*. Also, the balance of *yang* and *yin* may change in a particular object. Of course, men are predominantly *yang*, women predominantly *yin*— and therefore definitely inferior! Good spirits are also *yang*, while evil spirits are *yin*.

A fourth fundamental element of Chinese religions is polytheism, or worship of various gods. Though the objects worshiped have varied in different periods of history, diversity has been maintained in the popular religion until modern times.

In ancient times the worship of earth or fertility deities was prominent. Mounds of earth located at the villages and capital cities, served as centers for worship. Gradually, the worship of heaven became popular. This worship centered in the rites performed at the capital city by the emperor as the "son of heaven."

Of constant importance, also, was the worship of spirits. In this animistic worship, the countless good spirits (*shen*) and demons (*kwei*) were gradually learned and named. All sorts of magic practices were necessary for right relations with the spirit world.

Ancestor worship was universally practiced. The welfare of the family was dependent upon proper care of the ancestors. The ancestral shrine was the center of family life, and the ancestral temple was the mark of the clan's solidarity. The emperor worshiped the ancestors of the ruling dynasty. Thus ancestor worship sustained a strong sense of social solidarity.

A fifth basic idea of early Chinese religions was the belief that the emperor was the "son of heaven," chosen by heaven and the people. The welfare of the realm depended upon his proper worship of the gods. He was really "on the spot," because national disaster was taken as evidence that the emperor was guilty of negligence or sin. In that case, he could be deposed and his dynasty overthrown.

II. Taoism

1. *The Founder*

According to tradition, the founder of Taoism was Lao Tzu, born about 604 B.C., in the present Honan Province, Central China. However, many modern scholars doubt whether this sage ever existed. If he did, and if tradition can be trusted, he was curator of the imperial archives. From immediate contact with government and scholarship, he developed a skeptical attitude toward both. He wrote down his convictions in a book called the Tao Te Ching. Then he rode off on a black ox, to be seen no more. Even if the rest about him is true, it is almost certain that this book was produced at a later date than the time of Lao Tzu.

2. *The Tao Te Ching*

At any rate, the foundations of philosophical Taoism are laid in the book Tao Te Ching ("Classic of the Way and Virtue"). Here is a distinctive concept of the Tao, going beyond its common understanding as the "way" which heaven follows and men in turn should follow. The Tao is indefinable: The Tao that can be expressed is not the eternal Tao; the name that can be named is not the eternal name." Thus reads the opening sentence of the Tao Te Ching.

So—to proceed with the impossible: The Tao is the indefinite ground of the universe, the changeless Being from which all being comes. Although unknowable in its essential being, the Tao is operative in the world of nature, and human beings may find harmony with the Tao and fulness of being. Knowledge of the Tao is by intuition. (Here one is reminded of Zen Buddhism, which is quite dependent upon Taoism for its origin and its basic insights.)

The ethic of the Tao Te Ching is based upon the concept

of the Tao as nonactive but irresistible. The idea is that in the presence of natural kindness, nonaggressiveness, and non-meddlesomeness, evil is rendered powerless. Therefore one should render good for good, and good for evil.

"That the weak overcomes the strong,
And the yielding overcomes the unyielding,
Everyone knows this,
But no one can translate it into action." [3]

The three jewels of character are: gentleness, manifesting strength in weakness; humility, by which the wise man is exalted; and frugality, by which one accumulates but only to give away. In politics, the theory is that the least government possible is the best.

3. *Taoist Religion*

Chinese scholars built upon the teachings in the book, Tao Te Ching, some profound philosophies with religious connotations. These teachings may have been religiously satisfying to philosophers, but no doubt they were too difficult for the masses to grasp. At any rate, Taoism descended to the level of magic and popular religion.

The Taoist teachers claimed that through the Tao one could overcome the destructive powers of nature—harmful wild beasts and the like. Therefore, they were interpreted as possessing miraculous powers. The mysterious Taoist hermits were believed to have found the elixir of immortality, the drink that rendered them immune from death.

Imperial sanction was given to Taoism as a religion in the seventh century A.D. Gradually deities developed, with a Taoist Trinity, of which Lao Tzu was one; Eight Immortals, or ascetics who have achieved immortality; and various other gods and spirits. Monasteries and temples, priests and popes, and heaven and hell were added, much of this no doubt due to the influence of Buddhism in China.

III. CONFUCIANISM

Confucius is considered to be the greatest teacher of China. Not only has he profoundly affected Chinese culture through the centuries but also the culture of most of East Asia.

1. *The Life of Confucius*

There is more certain knowledge about Confucius than about Lao Tzu; but even so, a great deal of reliance must be placed upon tradition. He was born in the province of Lu, about 551 B.C. He was a semiorphan and was acquainted with poverty, but he received a superior upbringing in keeping with his aristocratic lineage. This included studies in classical literature and music.

After some years of minor political service and teaching, Confucius became a cabinet official of the Duke of Lu. Victimized by intrigue, he resigned at the age of fifty-five. For several years he wandered from province to province seeking a governmental post and giving gratuitous counsel to rulers. Finally, at the age of sixty-seven he was invited back to Lu, where he spent the rest of his life in honorable retirement, until his death in 479 B.C.

Tradition has credited Confucius with the production of the Five Confucian Classics, in part compiling and in part composing. But this is disputed by modern critical scholarship. His teaching is thought to be more certainly conveyed through the four books produced by his disciples.

2. *The Teaching of Confucius*

There is some doubt concerning the religious attitude of Confucius. He urged careful observance of the religious rites concerning gods and ancestors, believing that the welfare of the state and the virtue of the people depended upon this. He had much to say about ritual but little about vital religion. Though apparently an agnostic, there is evidence that Confucius had faith in the moral nature of the universe. In that faith, he was following a basic concept in Chinese religion, that heaven is not necessarily personal but moral.

This faith gave Confucius poise and confidence. He felt that heaven was back of him. In a time of discouragement he remarked that, although nobody knew him, perhaps, after all, he was known by heaven. And in a time when his life was in jeopardy, he asked if heaven was for him what could his enemies do to him? But, unlike the Taoists, he was not concerned with ultimate Reality, but with ethics.

Confucius' ethics were based upon this religious attitude, coupled with a conviction that man is basically good. What man needs is proper environment and, especially, right example. Therefore, in applying ethics to politics, the relation of ruler to subject is exalted. The moral example of a virtuous ruler is of utmost importance.

But Confucius taught that there are five cardinal relationships, of which that of sovereign and subject is but the first. The other four are relation of father and son, of elder and younger brothers, of husband and wife, and of friend and friend (or elder and junior). In each case there is the relationship of superior and inferior which is fundamental to feudal society. But the moral responsibility and good example of the superior is fully as important as the obedience of the inferior. At the very heart of the Confucian system is filial loyalty and piety which has made for the great strength of the family in China.

There are several key ideas expressing the Confucian ethic. Among these are propriety, humaneness, and reciprocity. The underlying principle is propriety. What is meant here is doing what is proper in relation to the moral order of the universe. Humaneness is like a law written upon the heart. Thus there is an internal and dynamic motivation which marks the "superior man." This may be so lofty that it is rarely seen, and Confucius seems not to have claimed it for himself;

but it is an ideal to which one must give reverence always.

The practical rule of reciprocity underlies human behavior. This law is to maintain balance and harmony in human relations. It means the "Golden Rule" of doing unto others as one would wish done to himself. But the principle of equity is not to be transgressed. So Confucius did not go as far as the Taoists and teach the returning of good for evil. Kindness is to be requited with kindness, but injury with justice.

3. *The Development of Confucianism*

Like Taoism, Confucianism inspired philosophical development, especially in the realms of the study of man, ethics, and political theory. In addition, Confucianism was adopted as the discipline and curriculum for the training of government officials. Thus, from the second century B.C., the civil service system was directed by Confucian teachers and Confucian ideals.

Confucianism also became a religion. The emperor honored Confucius and erected Confucian temples in the various provinces of China. In these temples, offerings were made to the spirit of Confucius. Ceremonies were observed, which became more and more elaborate, until they were simplified by a reform of the sixteenth century. "We may conclude by saying that Confucianism is not a religion in the fullest sense . . .; but it is generally so considered, and it at least has functioned as a religion in China."[4]

IV. POPULAR RELIGION

The religion of the masses is not exclusively Confucian, Taoist, or Buddhist. Worship may be performed at a temple belonging to one of these religions, but the temple itself may reflect the influence of the other two. What is more important is that folk religion, which is animistic and polytheistic, underlies the worship of the masses, wherever performed. In addition, there are religious rites in the home and at shrines outside the home. These rites honor ancestors, as well as certain gods and mythical creatures that do not exactly fit into the category of any of the three religions.

Especially prominent is the belief in innumerable spirits. Various superstitious and magical practices are used to insure good relations with the spirits. For example, images of gods may be carried in processions through the streets of a village to ward off evil spirits. Or certain written Chinese characters may be used for this purpose.

Closely related is a complex divination process. It is based upon the idea that in determining building sites, grave locations, and the like, one must reckon with mysterious forces lurking in these sites to act upon their inhabitants for good or ill. There are other forms of divination, fortunetelling, attention to probabilities of luck, and such, though there is some question whether these should be considered religious.

Dr. Wing-tsit Chan has suggested that instead of dividing the religious life of the Chinese into the three compartments of Taoism, Buddhism, and Confucianism, it should be seen on two levels: the level of the masses and that of the enlightened. The masses are the 85 per cent of the people who are "devout but ignorant." The enlightened are not only the "intelligentsia," but even illiterates who express "wisdom."

"The masses worship thousands of idols and natural objects of ancient, Buddhist, Taoist, and other origins, making special offering to whatever deity is believed to have the power to influence their lives at the time. The enlightened, on the other hand, honor only Heaven, ancestors, and sometimes also Confucius, Buddha, Lao Tzu, and a few great historical beings but not other spirits. . . . The masses believe in . . . varieties of superstitions. The enlightened are seldom contaminated by these diseases. The masses visit temples and shrines of all descriptions. The enlightened avoid these places, except the Temple of Heaven, ancestral halls, the

Confucian temple, and occasionally the temples of great historical personages. . . . The masses follow the beliefs and practices of the three systems and join various religious societies, with Taoism as the center. . . . The enlightened, on the other hand, follow the three systems primarily as philosophies, with Confucianism as the center." [5]

V. THE PRESENT SITUATION

What has happened to Chinese religion under the Communist domination of China?

First of all, it should be noted that much of religion was in serious decline before the Communists gained control. This was largely due to the modernization of China, prominent in this century, and by which the Chinese Republic was brought into being in 1911. The degraded magic of Taoism could not stand the impact of modern education. For all practical purposes, this religion was dead before the Communist revolution. Confucianism as a state cult was not maintained by the Republic and therefore was languishing. The temples were largely abandoned or taken over for nonreligious uses. Buddhism, also, had suffered by China's internal revolution and by the wars preceding the Communist coup.

However, not all Chinese religion was dying before the Communists took over. Certainly, the religion of the masses was seriously deteriorating, and traditional religious beliefs among the educated were being discarded. But it is also true that Chinese intellectuals had been showing an increasing interest in religion, especially in terms of its philosophic content. So philosophy, as related to the three prominent religions, was somewhat reviving. Moreover, Islam was holding its own (there are perhaps 25,000,000 or 30,000,000 adherents of Islam in China), and Christianity was growing.

Into this situation came the victory of communism with its hostile, or at least negative, attitude toward religion. The Communist regime, in the Common Principles of the People's

Republic, guaranteed freedom of religion. On the other hand, in keeping with communism's basic tenet that religion is the opiate of the people, a materialistic, atheistic attitude was encouraged and religion met with serious handicaps.

So far as Christianity is concerned, the "foreign" missionary work is completely ended. Most Christian institutions and properties of the churches have been confiscated by the Communist Government. A shift of leadership of the churches was effected to bring them largely under Communist control. Denominational identities have been, to significant degree, eliminated. Communes and required labor have disrupted church life, and leaders have been brainwashed.

In the small cities the usual practice has been to merge all the congregations into one, while in large cities they have been drastically reduced. For instance, in Peking it is said that the sixty-five churches of the city have been merged into four!

There is evidence also that Moslems have suffered persecution.

The concern here, however, is with Chinese religions—Taoism, Confucianism, Buddhism (because of its long tenure in China), and the more diffused religion of the masses. The lack of well-structured organization rendered Chinese religions especially vulnerable to the onslaught of communism.

Taoism, as a religious cult, was already practically dead, as we have noted, and now it appears completely extinct. Confucianism, likewise, as a religion seems to have disappeared. Such local Confucian temples and shrines as were still existing were taken over by the Communists and converted into schools or storage depots or put to some other such practical use.

Chinese Buddhism has been stripped of its temples, priesthood, and income, and largely of its influence. At the same time, the Communists utilized Buddhism for propaganda purposes. A Communist-inspired Chinese Buddhist Association was used to allay fears of the Buddhist countries of Asia that communism was an enemy of Buddhism.[6]

There are evidences also that the religion of the intellectuals—that is, the philosophies based on the three Chinese religions—is having rough sledding. Some non-Christian, as well as Christian, intellectuals have been brainwashed to conform to the Communist ideals. One of the major leaders of a Confucianist revival, in a public "confession" repudiated his whole system of philosophy and professed discipleship to Marx-Leninism and Mao Tse-tung. So, even the future of the philosophical foundations of Chinese culture is in grave uncertainty. However, many have faith that Confucianism, Taoism, and Buddhism will survive in some form.

The effect of communism upon the religion of the masses may be illustrated from a sociological study of a Chinese village. This study was accomplished by field research, 1948-51, and continued by gleanings from the Communist and non-Communist press.[7]

The village was Nanching, near Canton. The population of Nanching was about 1100, divided into about 230 households. Institutional religion was represented by the Taoist temple of the god of fire, with one Taoist priest, and by a village seeress who had a private altar in her home and a professionalized practice.

Villagers had no permanent or exclusive connection to this temple or priest. They worshiped in temples of other villages or towns, if occasion or convenience required. The villagers also worshiped at ancestral halls of the village clans, the elders comprising the priesthood. Moreover, they participated in peasant cults, represented, for example, by a small altar to the god of earth and grain standing at the center of the village.

Now, what happened when the Communists gained control of the village? The temple of the god of fire remained unmolested, except that most of its land was redistributed. The peasants were given some of the land and a share was retained for the priest. He had to farm his allotment to make a living, since his income from the rent of the land was cut off. The seeress was given a share of the land from the land reform. She was charged by the officials with fraud and urged to give up her superstitious practices. Confiscation of clan lands curtailed clan ceremonies, but ancestor worship continued in the families. Religious festivals in honor of the gods were so consistently discouraged by the Communist authorities that the village had abandoned them by 1950.

"In general . . . the early impact of Communism on religion in Nanching pretty well typified official Communist policy. . . . By the impoverishment of rich families and the clans, religion was, so to speak, driven from public view back into the homes, where the unchangeable older generation of peasants could cherish their traditional customs and beliefs undisturbed. But the power of religion to strengthen community spirit and to evoke a sense of community sharing was already nearly destroyed. Most important of all, the Communists had embarked on a long-term program . . . aimed at the eradication of traditional religious influence in Chinese life. At the heart of that program was the education of the younger generation. . . . The outcome of this vastly ambitious plan was a question for the future." [8]

What about the survival of religion in China? It is a "question for the future." At the present, religion seems to have a better hope of survival among Chinese outside Red China distributed in other Asiatic countries.

Taiwan (Formosa) is the seat of the government of Free China or Nationalistic China. The population, except for some mountain tribes, is almost entirely Chinese in origin, either from recent or older immigration. The people of Hong Kong and Macao, likewise, are predominantly Chinese. Hong Kong's population is greatly swollen by a stream of refugees from Communist China.

In addition, there are Chinese minorities of significant dimensions in the countries of Southeast Asia. For example, over one third of Malaya's people are Chinese, perhaps 3,000,000 of Thailand's, and 2,000,000 of Indonesia's. They tend not to integrate themselves into the national life of these countries but rather to retain their separate cultural identity.

In these communities of Chinese one can find the religion of pre-Communist China continuing—unfortunately with much of its superstitions. The ancestral cult is much in evidence and the ancestral tablets are carefully preserved. Perhaps this cult is fortified by the tenacious clinging to Chinese identity and the resistance to cultural assimilation. Buddhist temples are well distributed, with the image of Kwan-yin, the goddess of mercy, prominent. These also serve as repositories for the ancestral tablets. Even here, however, skepticism is growing—due, no doubt, to secularistic influences in general, and possibly in part to the influence of communism.

Over the religions of China hangs a giant question mark. Though we shall not mourn the passing of their superstition and baser elements, we may hope that the wisdom of this ancient people shall not be lost to the world. And especially we desire its preservation in the circle of commitment to him who alone is the Truth, the Way, and the Life. Confucius is great, but a Greater than Confucius is here!

FOR CLASS DISCUSSION

1. What are the fundamental concepts of Chinese religion?
2. Compare Confucianism and Taoism.
3. How is Communist domination affecting religion in China?
4. Describe the religious situation of Chinese communities outside China.

NOTES

[1] Noss, *Man's Religions,* p. 293. Used by permission of The Macmillan Company.

[2] Y. C. Yang, *China's Religious Heritage* (New York: Abingdon-Cokesbury Press, 1943), pp. 40–41. Used by permission of Abingdon Press.

[3] Tao Te Ching, 78, in *Sources of Chinese Tradition,* comp. Wm. Theodore de Bary *et al.* (New York: Columbia University Press, 1960), p. 63. Used by permission of Columbia University Press.

[4] Yang, *op. cit.,* p. 60.

[5] Wing-tsit Chan, *Religious Trends in Modern China* (New York: Columbia University Press, 1953), pp. 142–143. Used by permission of Columbia University Press.

[6] *Cf.* Chang-tu Hu *et al., China: Its People, Its Society, Its Culture* (New Haven: Human Relations Area Files Press, 1960), pp. 130–133.

[7] C. K. Yang, *A Chinese Village in Early Communist Transition* (Cambridge: The Technology Press, 1959), esp. pp. 191 ff. Used by permission of the M.I.T. Press.

[8] *Ibid.,* pp. 195–196.

JUDAISM

I. THE JEW AND HIS WORSHIP PRACTICES
1. From Birth Until Death
2. The Sabbath
3. Other Holy Days and Festivals
4. Holy Things and Symbols

II. THE TRAGIC COURSE OF JEWISH HISTORY
1. The Beginnings of Judaism
2. The Shifting Centers of Jewish Life
3. "Despised and Rejected of Men"

III. THE JEW IN THE WORLD OF TODAY
1. Where Are the Jews?
2. The Types of Judaism
3. Other Jewish Movements
4. How Do You Define "Jew"?
5. The Mystery of Jewish Continuity

IV. THE CHRISTIAN ATTITUDE TOWARD THE JEW

6

Judaism

As CHRISTIANS we share with the Jews a common background. Our own faith has its roots in the religion of the ancient Jews. We share with them the Scriptures which we call the Old Testament. So when we turn from the religions of East Asia to Judaism, we are on familiar ground—or are we? Do we really know who the Jew is? Do we know his religious practices and attitudes? Do we know his history?

I. THE JEW AND HIS WORSHIP PRACTICES

1. *From Birth Until Death*

Like most religions, Judaism involves its adherents in religious rites from birth until death. Special naming ceremonies are held for the girl baby in the house of worship during a service and for the boy infant at the time of circumcision. At the age of five the children are enrolled in schools to educate them in their faith. These schools usually meet on Saturday or on Sunday mornings, but sometimes on weekday afternoons as well. Jewish children attend these schools in addition to public school. In some cases, they attend Jewish parochial schools.

Confirmation in synagogue or temple membership involves special ceremonies by which the boy becomes *bar mitzvah* or "son of the Commandment," and the girl becomes *bat mitzvah* or "daughter of the Commandment." In addition, there are religious services for marriage, ordination to the ministry as a rabbi (teacher), and the funeral.

2. *The Sabbath*

The Jewish sabbath is from sunset on Friday until sunset on Saturday. The sabbath is revered with profound religious feeling, almost as though it has a personality. It is welcomed as a queen or bride. It is a day for worship, relaxation, and learning. Just before twilight on Friday, the mother of the Jewish household lights candles and says a prayer. By this means she welcomes the sabbath queen or bride into the house. The candlelight warms the hearts of the family assembled around the festive table and everybody feels good. The father lifts the cup of wine and recites the *Kiddush* or blessing: "Blessed art thou, O Lord our God, King of the universe, who hast created the fruit of the vine." Then the family join in a prayer of thanksgiving, after which the father takes a piece of special sabbath bread and shares it with the family. Obviously, this sabbath dinner has great significance for family unity.

Services follow in the synagogue or temple on Friday evening. These consist of a ceremony of welcoming the sabbath similar to that observed in the home, a call to worship and the recitation of prayers, singing or chanting, reading of the Law or Torah, sermon and benediction. The prayers include the *Shema,* the powerful confession of the oneness of God recorded in Deuteronomy 6:4 ff.; the *Amidah,* or "standing" prayers (though in Reform temples the congregation remains seated for these seven prayers); and the *Kaddish,* or memorial prayer for departed loved ones.

Services may also be held on Saturday morning in synagogue or temple. Classes may be conducted on Saturday afternoon for study of the Scriptures and the Talmud. Or the Jew may study or relax at home.

With twilight on Saturday evening the members of the Jewish household bid the sabbath queen or bride farewell with a fitting ceremony and wish each other and their friends a "good week."

3. *Other Holy Days and Festivals*

In addition to the weekly round of holy sabbath days, there are seven other special holy days or seasons during the year. The dates vary because the Jewish calendar is lunar and differs from ours.

Rosh Hashanah is the Jewish New Year which comes sometime in September. It is followed ten days later with the solemn observance of the Yom Kippur, or "Day of Atonement." In October (usually) come the nine days of Succoth, or "Feast of Tabernacles," which is a thanksgiving festival.

Hanukkah, the "Feast of Lights," occurs near the end of November or in December. It commemorates the freedom won for the Jews when the Jewish Maccabees overthrew the Syrian oppressors during the interbiblical period. Therefore it is a festival of independence, observed for eight days. The "Feast of Lots," or Purim, is another victory holiday. Celebrated for one day in February or March, it is in remembrance of the salvation of the Jews from the wicked Haman of Persia, as related in the book of Esther.

Pesach, the "Passover," is observed in late March or April, commemorating the deliverance or "exodus" from Egypt. This great festival, along with the other feasts of deliverance or victory, helps to nurture messianic hopes. At Passover, an empty chair and a glass of wine are provided at the family table for Elijah, in hope that he will come and bring the Messiah.

"Pentecost," or Shabuoth, comes fifty days after Passover begins, which means the end of May or early June. It is a festival of the ingathering of late spring harvest and also a celebration of the receiving of the Ten Commandments at the hand of Moses, who is supposed to have come down from Mount Sinai with the two tables of stone on Pentecost day.

4. *Holy Things and Symbols*

The central shrine of worship in the temple or synagogue is the ark where the scrolls of the Torah, or Law, are kept. The Torah consists of the first five books of the Bible: Genesis, Exodus, Leviticus, Numbers, and Deuteronomy. The ark is a beautifully built cabinet, accompanied on each side by a seven-branched candelabra or *menorah*. Thus the sabbath worship makes central the Torah, which is the first and most important division of Jewish Scriptures.

The other divisions of the Jewish Scriptures are the "Prophets" and the "Writings." But to the devout Jew, the Torah is life itself. Often the tablets of the Ten Commandments are placed above the ark; and in front of these is the *Ner Tamid* or "Eternal Light." It is kept burning as a reminder of the eternity of God and the perpetuity of the Jewish way of life.

The Talmud also is in the category of sacred literature. It consists of sixty-three volumes in six major parts, compiled over a long period of time, culminating about the end of the fifth century A.D. The Talmud brings together teachings and biblical interpretations of the rabbis, and traditions for the ordering of Jewish life.

From the instructions in the *Shema*, Deuteronomy 6:4–9, other symbols or objects of devotion have originated. The *tefilin*, or phylacteries, fulfil the command: "And thou shalt bind them [these words] for a sign upon thine hand, and they shall be as frontlets between thine eyes." The *tefilin* are two square leather boxes with straps. One of the boxes is fastened to the forehead and the other to the left arm. Inside the *tefilin* are certain passages from the Torah, including the *Shema*.

The *mezuzah* is used in response to the command to "write them upon the posts of thy house, and on thy gates." The *mezuzah* is a metal or wood case containing the first two sections of the *Shema* written on a parchment. It is fastened on the doorpost or doors of the Jewish house to remind the family of their responsibility toward God.

The *tallith* is a tasseled prayer shawl having its origin in a commandment found in Numbers 15:37–39. It is given to the Jewish boy at his confirmation rites. All male Jews wear the prayer shawls during worship at Conservative or Orthodox synagogues.

A familiar symbol is the *Mogen David*, "Shield of David" or "Star of David." This is a star formed by two interlocking triangles.

II. THE TRAGIC COURSE OF JEWISH HISTORY

1. *The Beginnings of Judaism*

Although Hebrew or Jewish religion dates back at least to the time of Moses for its origins, what is identifiable as "Judaism" comes much later. Scholars usually see its beginnings in the period after the exile when the Jews returned to Jerusalem from Babylon in a series of migrations beginning in 538 B.C. About a century later under Ezra and Nehemiah the structure of Judaism was completed. New furnishings would be added from time to time, but the building had been erected.

The religion of Judaism which Ezra and Nehemiah established, was quite legalistic. Its chief leaders were priests, and its infallible guide was the book of the Law (Torah). It was concerned with ritual and ceremonial cleanliness. It emphasized careful obedience to scriptural law. It was racially as well as religiously exclusive.[1]

2. *The Shifting Centers of Jewish Life*

Judaism's center continued in Palestine with developments under Greek and Roman domination and with a period of Maccabean independence sandwiched in between. Then, after the Christian era had dawned, the seething emotions and messianic expectations erupted in Jewish rebellion against the Romans. The result was the slaughter, horrible beyond description, which accompanied the destruction of Jerusalem by Titus in A.D. 70. This was followed by dispersion of the Jews throughout the ancient world. But the center of Jewish intellectual strength continued in Palestine until the fourth or fifth century.

Gradually, however, Jewish intellectual life in Babylonia gained the ascendancy and so a new center developed. It was here that the compilation of the Talmud, which had been started in Palestine, was finished by the end of the fifth century A.D.

Meanwhile, a large Jewish community had emerged in Spain. Following the capture of Spain by Moslems in the early part of the eighth century, a golden age of Jewish history came about in that country. Moslems were fairly lenient to the Jews. Jewish literature, philosophy, and theology began to flourish.

After Spain once more came into Christian hands, persecution of the Jews intensified. Jewish cultural progress went into an eclipse from which it was not to emerge until the modern period.

Now the important center of Jewish life is America, with a possible shift to the state of Israel in progress.

3. *"Despised and Rejected of Men"*

Allusions have already been made to persecution of the Jews. In the early period, Jewish rebellions against Roman rule in Palestine were followed by oppressive measures against the Jews. In Babylonia, from the third century A.D., they were persecuted by Zoroastrians, until Moslem conquest gave them some relief.

Unfortunately, Jews suffered longest and most in the professedly Christian countries of Europe. Christian hostility toward the Jews was sustained by the adamant Jewish refusal of Christianity and by the memory that "the Jews crucified Jesus." However, the more accurate statement is that "the human race crucified Jesus." At any rate, Christians proceeded to crucify him anew by persecuting his brethren according to the flesh.

Under the Christian Roman Empire the Jews suffered harsh treatment. As they scattered into the growing nation states of Europe, they continued to meet with Christian hostility. In turn, this hostility bred increasing Jewish separateness and seclusion.

The Crusades, beginning in A.D. 1095 with the main purpose of wresting the Holy Land from "infidel" Moslem hands, ushered in a new period of persecution of the Jews. Crusaders found diversion on their way to the Holy Land by massacring Jews in Germany and Eastern Europe.

In many nations of Europe the choice became conversion to Christianity or expulsion. Legally, the Jews were expelled from England in 1290, from France in 1394, and from Spain in 1492. In Spain, the Inquisition ferreted out Jews (and Moslems) who were suspected of falsely converting to Christianity. Jews fled to Poland in the north and to the Moslem countries in the east.

In places in Europe where they remained, such as Germany, the Jews were required to live in segregated quarters called *ghettos*. These ghettos were usually in the inferior parts of the towns. The Jews were compelled to wear an identifying "Jew Badge," or patch, on their garments, and to remain within their ghettos at night. The result, understandably, was a "ghetto mentality," a defensive and separatist attitude by which the Jews came to approve of their isolation from the world about them. Terrible "pogroms" or massacres, such as the slaughter of a half million Jews by the Cossacks in seventeenth-century Poland, must have strengthened this mentality.

Only gradually did the Jews effect transition to the modern

world, with its ideals of toleration and freedom. Prominent in this transition were the American and French revolutions in the last quarter of the eighteenth century. America, especially, became the land of great opportunity for the Jew. Almost one half of the total world Jewish population is now found in the United States.

Moreover, through the leadership of great men like Moses Mendellsohn (1729–1786) of Germany, the Jew was freed from the ghetto mentality and took his place in the world of culture. The result has been remarkable contributions by Jews to various phases of modern development—in science, art, literature, and other areas.

Even so, the Jew was by no means through with persecution. In fact, the worst was yet to come. The world has been shocked beyond expression by the attempt of the madman Adolf Hitler to exterminate the Jews. It is estimated that 6,000,000 Jews, one half of their present world population, were murdered by this fanatic and his associates and their racist policies. And no doubt the end is not yet, for anti-Semitism (hatred and prejudice against the Jew) still rears its ugly head.

III. THE JEW IN THE WORLD OF TODAY

1. *Where Are the Jews?*

How many Jews do you think there are in the world's nearly 3,000,000,000 people today? Chances are you overestimated, for there are only about 12,000,000. This is a tiny minority indeed, isn't it? That such a small group could be so prominent and create such difficult problems is testimony to the mystery and significance of the Jewish people.

The Jews are scattered throughout the world. About 1,600,000 are in the new nation of Israel. But over 5,000,000—almost half of the total—are in the United States. The largest single community of Jews in the world is in New York City, where there are over 2,000,000—a larger Jewish population than in Israel.

2. *The Types of Judaism*

There are three religious groupings of Jewish people in the United States, and these divisions obtain to some measure elsewhere. There is considerable co-operation between these groups, and they are not usually termed denominations.

(1) *Reform Judaism* developed in Germany over a century ago as an attempt to adjust this ancient faith to the modern world. It has abbreviated rituals and holy seasons and has translated liturgies into languages of the various countries where Jews are found. Reform Judaism has further revolutionized Jewish worship by allowing families to sit together at worship and making the wearing of hats at worship optional. Its places of worship are sometimes called temples instead of synagogues. It makes no emphasis upon dietary laws and many Reform Jews have discarded them.

Reform Judaism has liberalized the doctrine of basic Judaism, while retaining the concept of Torah. Belief in the coming of a personal Messiah is not included, and instead of resurrection there is a doctrine of immortality. Followers of Reform Judaism believe in Judaism as a true religion, but not necessarily the only true religion. It is open to new findings of science and progressive movements of religion and culture.

The 520 congregations of Reform Judaism co-operate in the Union of American Hebrew Congregations, with headquarters moved recently from Cincinnati to New York. The companion body of this organization is the Central Conference of American Rabbis.

(2) *Orthodox Judaism* reacted vigorously against the Reform movement. It has insisted upon the finality and completeness of the ancient Torah. It has held tenaciously to the requirements of the Talmud concerning worship

practices, dietary laws, and the observance of the holidays.

Even in this group, however, some concessions to modern life are being made. In some congregations the sexes are not segregated and English sermons are common. Some leniency in dietary regulations is appearing also. Hope for a personal Messiah is maintained, as is also the belief in resurrection.

Of special interest is the growth of the Jewish version of parochial schools which Orthodox Judaism sponsors. These are attended by about 30,000 Jewish children. The Union of Orthodox Jewish Congregations of America, with offices in New York, has more than seven hundred congregations in the United States and Canada. Many other Orthodox congregations are unaffiliated. There is more than one Rabbinical Council.

(3) *Conservative Judaism* is a reaction against what were considered the excesses of Reform Judaism. It is a middle-of-the-road movement between Orthodoxy and Reform. Its main principles may be stated thus: change and adjustment are inevitable, but within this change the essential continuity of Judaism in all places must be retained. It reports 508 congregations in the United Synagogue of America, located in New York. Its rabbis are organized in the Rabbinical Assembly of America, with a membership of six hundred.

3. *Other Jewish Movements*

There are other important movements in Judaism that cut across the lines of these three groupings.

(1) *Reconstructionism* does not aim at producing separate congregations, though a few have emerged. It aims to adjust Jewish life to the modern situation in a way apparently more radical than Reform Judaism. It views religion as a functional aspect of culture or civilization. The attitude of Reconstructionism is reflected in the title of a book by Mordecai M. Kaplan, its founder: *Judaism Without Supernaturalism.*

(2) *Zionism* is a modern movement founded upon the

perpetual yearning of Jews to return to what they considered their homeland in Palestine, centering in the Holy City, Jerusalem (Zion). The movement was founded by Theodor Herzl (1860–1904). He believed that the only solution to the problem of the Jew in a more or less hostile world was the permission to form a Jewish state in Palestine. The first Zionist Congress, which convened in Basle, Switzerland in 1897, organized the movement and set forth its program. The program included the encouraging of emigration to Palestine of Jewish artisans, agriculturists, and craftsmen. It advocated the strengthening of Jewish national consciousness and efforts to procure the assent of governments to the creation of a Jewish national state.

The problems for Jews in the twentieth century, and especially the brutal massacres of Jews by the Nazis, helped convince various political leaders of the validity of a Jewish state. The result was the establishment of the state of Israel, May 14, 1948. Thus the aim of Zionism was accomplished. However, Israel's existence in an Arab world has fanned ancient animosities between Jew and Arab to flame, and very difficult and controversial issues remain unsettled. The Zionist movement has continued. It now has the modified purpose of strengthening the state of Israel, encouraging further emigration to this Jewish homeland, and fostering the unity of the Jewish people.

4. *How Do You Define* "*Jew*"?

Anyone who thinks this question is easy to answer cannot answer it! And maybe no one else can!

(1) Obviously, one cannot define the Jew by the category of "race." Commonly Jews are referred to as "Semitic," but there are other Semites who are not Jews, such as the Arabs. Also, there are many Jews who are not Semites. The Jews never have been a "pure race," and modern Jewry is composed of many races.

(2) Neither will "religion" serve as an adequate category to describe the Jews. Many of them are irreligious but yet cling to their identity as Jews. Judaism is more concerned with *doing* than *believing*. It has never been a dogmatic faith. Piety and faith are expressed in obedience to prescribed regulations much more than in creed. If there were theological doctrines or beliefs, these were the lofty conception of God as one and holy, the creation of man in God's image, the revelation of God in history, the authority of the Torah, the election of Israel as God's special people, and the hope of a Messiah.

But the simple truth is that Judaism today has become highly secularized. This is certainly the case in America where almost half of world Jewry is found. It is true in some significant measure elsewhere.

Both in terms of doctrine and practice many Jews have traveled far from religious Judaism. It is a long distance indeed from the majestic vision of God's sovereign holiness of Isaiah 6 to Mordecai M. Kaplan's concept of God. He describes God as "the Power that makes for salvation," or "that aspect of the cosmos that makes for man's salvation," or "the creative principle at work in the cosmos." [2] However, Kaplan believes that his "reconstruction" of Judaism is an alternative to secularism. A Jewish sociologist has declared that if a very careful survey of all the American Jews were taken, "We would find only a small minority who, asked about the nature of their religious beliefs, would respond with a declaration of faith in the authority of the law, the providence of God, Israel's election, and the coming of the Messiah." [3]

So far as the practice of Jewish faith is concerned, the traditional pattern has largely been abandoned and replaced by conformity to secular American culture. In some ways, Jews have become more secularized than other American religious groups. A survey conducted in the early 1950's showed 50 per cent of American Jews indicating active synagogue membership, as compared with 87 per cent of Catholics and 75 per cent of Protestants indicating active church membership.[4]

Other polls reported attendance at worship services at least once a month by 83 per cent of the Catholics and 65 per cent of the Protestants, but only 18 per cent of the Jews. A Jewish writer referred to these polls to substantiate his claim that the abandonment of the faith and practice of religion in America is far more widespread among Jews than Christians.[5]

Yet, recently there have been indications of a "return to the synagogue" and a growing understanding of the Jewish community as "religious," though the concept of religion involved may be quite secular. What is more important, no doubt, is the fact that the Jews insist on remaining Jews. They may pay no attention to the Jewish law and know nothing of their Jewish faith. Nevertheless, for the most part, they do not completely cast off the yoke of the Jewish heritage.

"The refusal to become non-Jews stems from an attitude of mind that seems to be . . . a stubborn insistence on remaining a Jew, enhanced by no particularly ennobling idea of what that means. And yet it has the effect of relating American Jews, let them be as ignorant of Judaism as a Hottentot, to a great religious tradition. Thus, the insistence of the Jews on remaining Jews, which may take the religiously indifferent forms of liking Yiddish jokes, supporting Israel, raising money for North African Jews, and preferring certain kinds of food, has a potentially religious meaning."[6]

Consequently, simply to classify the Jews in terms of religion, or to explain their distinctiveness purely on religious grounds, is only half truth, to say the least.

(3) Likewise, to refer to the Jews as a "nation," as does Nathan Glazer,[7] is misleading. They do not occupy one "contiguous stretch of territory." Of course, the inhabitants

of Israel are a nation; but not all of them are Jews, and the vast majority of Jews in the world are not citizens of Israel. Rather, they are a dispersed people.

(4) Perhaps the best one can do is call them a "people" —along with Robert Gordis, who is one of them.

"The only term which is sufficiently inclusive to be used to describe the Jews is the old Biblical word '*am*, meaning 'a people,' from a Semitic root probably connoting 'togetherness.' Jews the world over differ in social outlook, political citizenship, economic status, and religious attitude. Yet the overwhelming majority are conscious of the fact that they are members of one people, sharing a common history and a sense of kinship inherited from the past, a common tradition and way of life in the present, and a common destiny and hope for themselves and for the world in the future." [8]

5. *The Mystery of Jewish Continuity*

The Jews are unique and there is mystery about their continuity. This mystery is a problem for Christians, and has been ever since the apostle Paul grappled with it in Romans 9 to 11. It certainly cannot be dealt with adequately in the limits of this discussion. Perhaps the following guidelines may be indicated, drawn from the New Testament, and centering in the passage in Romans just mentioned:

(1) There is but one "Israel" of God, which is neither Jewish nor Gentile but is above race and above nation (Rom. 9:6–8; Col. 3:11; Eph. 2:11–22; and Gal. 3:27–29).

(2) Membership in this true Israel is determined by faith in Israel's Messiah (Christ) who is Jesus the Lord (Rom. 10:1–13; 11:17–24).

(3) Christ is the hope of ancient Israel and the chief cornerstone of the true Israel. This Stone is judgment upon those rejecting him but is "precious" to those who receive him (Rom. 9:30–33; 1 Pet. 2:4–10).

(4) In his mysterious sovereignty, God has an *immediate*

purpose of mercy in the "hardening" of ancient Israel by which they refuse the Messiah (Rom. 11:11–12, 25, 30–32).

(5) But God's *ultimate* purpose for his ancient people Israel can be fulfilled only as they are brought to faith in the Messiah and thus joined to his Body, which is the true Israel and the one people of God (Rom. 9:1–5; 10:1; 11:26–29).

IV. THE CHRISTIAN ATTITUDE TOWARD THE JEW

The Jews are distributed among us here in America as our fellow Americans. What should be our attitude toward them? Of course, our primary responsibility is to *love* them. As Christians we are to love all people. But this responsibility has a special meaning with reference to the Jews. We must love them because they are non-Christians with whom we are in immediate contact, because we share with them the common heritage of Old Testament religion, and because our Lord was a Jew. But most of all we must love them because of the centuries of persecution of Jews at the hands of Christians.

"The recent slaughter of six million Jews should prey upon our Christian conscience. . . . The atrocities compounded upon the Jews by Hitler and the Nazi regime grew from the scattered seeds of anti-Semitism which found fertile soil in almost every Christian heart. The Nazi terror returns a resounding echo of every brutal remark we have allowed our children to make to Jewish children, every silence we have maintained in the face of Jewish quotas in our colleges and universities, every refusal to expose and oppose restricted sale of real estate which intends to 'keep our neighborhoods free of Jews,' every Christian sermon which by its ambiguity has laid responsibility for the Crucifixion of our Lord upon our Jewish contemporaries." [9]

Our attitude of love must incorporate that profound repentance which can never be adequately expressed.

Similarly, our attitude should be one of genuine friendliness. The Jew will not respond favorably to an approach to him that smacks of self-interest. He is repelled by the thought that he may be a contemplated notch on the gunhandle of a Christian's personal evangelism. Indeed, the best evangelism toward the Jew is sometimes just plain Christian friendship which accepts him as he is.

Finally, however, we are to pray and work under the Holy Spirit's direction for the conversion of the Jew to faith in Jesus Christ. This requires patience, tact, understanding, sympathy, and much love. But, working together with God, we may see walls of prejudice and suspicion and rejection disintegrating before love. And we may see foregleams of that day when "all Israel shall be saved"—including the "part of Israel" now hardened. In short, we may hope to win the Jews to faith in their Messiah and ours and inclusion among his people—only as we *are and behave like* his people to them.

FOR CLASS DISCUSSION

1. Does Judaism have basic doctrines? If so, what are they, and are they important to Jews?
2. What is mysterious about the continued existence of the Jews as a distinct people?
3. Does God have a purpose for the Jews which is independent of his purpose for the church?
4. What is the Christian attitude toward the Jew?

NOTES

[1] Noss, *Man's Religions*, pp. 515–516.

[2] Mordecai M. Kaplan, *Judaism Without Supernaturalism* (New York: The Reconstructionist Press, 1958), pp. 119–120. Used by permission of The Reconstructionist Press.

[3] Nathan Glazer, *American Judaism* (Chicago: The University of Chicago Press, 1957), p. 130. Copyright 1957 by the University of Chicago. Used by permission of the University of Chicago Press.

[4] Will Herberg, *Protestant, Catholic, Jew* (New York: Doubleday and Company, 1955), pp. 210, 223.

[5] Robert Gordis, *Judaism for the Modern Age* (New York: Farrar, Straus and Cudahy, 1955), pp. 28–29. Used by permission of Farrar, Straus and Cudahy, Inc.

[6] Glazer, *op. cit.*, pp. 141–142.

[7] *Ibid.*, p. 3.

[8] Gordis, *op. cit.*, p. 47.

[9] Perry, *The Gospel in Dispute*, p. 140. Copyright 1958 by Edmund Perry. Reprinted by permission of Doubleday and Company, Inc.

ISLAM

I. Definitions and Distribution

II. The Life of Mohammed

III. Expansion and Development
   1. The Conquests
   2. The Crusades
   3. Christians Under Moslem Rule
   4. Sectarian Divisions and Orthodoxy

IV. The Faith and Conduct of the Moslem
   1. Fundamental Beliefs
   2. The Code of Conduct

V. Contemporary Islam
   1. Factors Producing Change
   2. Reactions to Modern Influences
   3. Missionary Revival
   4. The Black Muslims

7

Islam

LIKE JUDAISM and Christianity, Islam is a religion originating in the Near East and among Semitic people. Moreover, like these religions of the Bible, it is strongly monotheistic and emphasizes a unique revelation from the one God. It shares much of Old Testament history and claims Abraham as its great patriarch. Moreover, it betrays some influences from Christianity.

I. DEFINITIONS AND DISTRIBUTION

Islam is the religion of over 400,000,000 people distributed over a vast area from Africa to the Far East.

"Islam" means "submission," so Islam is the religion of submission to the will of God. "Moslem" comes from the same Arabic word as Islam and means "a submitter" or "one who submits" to God. This religion is sometimes called "Mohammedanism" and its adherents "Mohammedans"; but Moslems resent these names and prefer Islam and Moslem. There are also different spellings for Moslem words, being variously transliterated from the Arabic. Thus "Moslem" may also be spelled "Muslim" or "Muslem." And "Mohammed" may be spelled "Muhammed" or "Muhammad."

The Arabic areas of North Africa and the Near East are almost solidly Moslem. The Turkish areas and Iran, also, are predominantly Moslem. Indonesia is the most populous Islamic country, and Pakistan is second in size. In addition, there are several million Moslems in China, as we have noticed, and many more in Malaya, the Philippines, and other

Far Eastern countries, as well as about 40,000,000 in India. Over 20,000,000 are in the Soviet Union and about 3,699,000 in the Balkan countries of Europe. It is estimated that there are 35,000,000 adherents of Islam in Africa south of the Sahara. Western countries include only about 800,000.

II. THE LIFE OF MOHAMMED

Non-Moslems usually consider the Prophet Mohammed as the founder of Islam. They also consider him responsible for the Moslem sacred scripture, the *Qur'an*, or Koran as Westerners call it. Moslems, however, prefer to call Mohammed God's Messenger and the interpreter and exemplar of the Koran, which is eternal.

Mohammed was born in Mecca, Arabia, in A.D. 571, of a leading tribe of the Arabs. His father died before his birth, and his mother died in his sixth year. He was then taken into his grandfather's house, and upon the latter's death he was reared by an uncle. As a youth, he lived in humble circumstances, working as a shepherd and an attendant on caravans. On these journeys he probably came into contact with Christians and Jews.

At the age of twenty-five, Mohammed married his rich employer, the widow Khadijah. Though his bride was fifteen years older than he, theirs seems to have been a love match. Polygamy was the order of the day, but Mohammed did not take another wife until after Khadijah's death, whereupon he married several.

Mohammed was probably illiterate, the Koran being written down by disciples who remembered his words. But he had a lively poetic imagination and mystic religious temperament.

When forty years of age, Mohammed began to experience visions by which he received his prophetic call. These came to him after a period of solitude in a mountain cave north of

Mecca. In the visions, the angel Gabriel appeared and convinced Mohammed that he was the messenger of God, known in Arabia as Allah. This conviction did not come until after a period of doubt during which Khadijah encouraged her husband to believe in his visions.

Instructed by Gabriel to proclaim God's message, Mohammed began to preach a strong monotheism, or belief in God, and a denunciation of the idolatrous polytheism (worship of many gods) and primitive religion of Arabia. His preaching provoked resentment and he and his followers left Mecca and moved to Medina, also in Arabia. The flight, or *Hegira*, in A.D. 622, is very important to Moslems, and their calendar dates from it.

In Medina, Mohammed was accepted as prophet and leader. Here he demonstrated the practical abilities which accompanied his religious genius by organizing an army. He defended Medina against attack by the Meccans, and finally, in 630, captured Mecca. He then proclaimed his mastery of Arabia and was able to make his claim stick before his sudden death in 632.

It has been suggested that Mohammed came into contact with Christians and Jews. Much has been made of the failure and corruption of Christianity as having given rise to Islam. How far these criticisms are justified is difficult to know. There are indications that the Christianity of the Near East was strongly ascetic and world-denying, having been influenced by Eastern religions, and that it was much given to image worship. If Mohammed actually knew this type of Christianity, it would have offended his strong opposition to idolatry.

In any event, there are evidences that Mohammed tragically misunderstood Christianity. In the Koran the idea of the Christian Trinity seems to be that of the Father, Jesus, and Mary. Jesus' virgin birth is affirmed, but his deity is strongly denied. The crucifixion, also, is denied, and there-fore, by implication, the resurrection.

III. EXPANSION AND DEVELOPMENT

The visions and revelations of Mohammed were recorded as the Koran which, along with the unwritten prophecies or *Sunnah,* became the basis for a new religion, militant and bent on conquering the world for God (Allah).

1. *The Conquests*

There are many passages in the Koran which exhort the faithful to do battle for the defense or advancement of God's religion, promising rewards for those who respond and penal-ties for those who refuse. So the "caliphs," or successors to Mohammed, made fanatical military campaigns to conquer the world in the name of Allah and his Prophet Mohammed. Within twenty-five years after the prophet's death they con-trolled an area larger than the Roman Empire!

By A.D. 795 they had conquered not only all the area of the Near East, but North Africa and Spain as well. By what appears now as a giant pincer movement, their armies threatened Europe, via Asia Minor in the east and Spain in the west. By two very strategic battles they were stopped. In 717–718 they were defeated by the Greek emperor, Leo III, as they beseiged Constantinople; and in 732 by Charles Martel, the Frankish leader, at the Battle of Tours as they spilled across the Pyrenees into France.

Within another century or so they penetrated into Central Asia and India, creating a Moslem kingdom which was to last for several centuries. Turks and Mongols erupted west-ward from Asia in the Middle Ages, adopting Islam as their faith and carving great empires. Constantinople finally fell to Moslem Turks in 1453, and the Turks penetrated into Europe.

2. *The Crusades*

Meantime the Crusades were conducted, 1095–1291, as an expression of medieval European Christianity and chivalry. Motives were:

To make pilgrimages to the Holy Land safe for the superstitious Christians of that era

To wrest the Holy Land from the hands of the Moslem "infidels"

To protect the Eastern Christian Roman Empire in Greece, the Balkans, and Asia Minor from the Turks

To encourage union between Christians of Western and Eastern Europe

Instead, the Crusades unleashed passions of cruelty, prejudice, adventure, and greed, as well as heroism and idealism on the part of Crusaders. The Holy Land was not permanently taken from the Moslems. The Eastern Roman Empire was weakened so that it succumbed to the Turks in 1453, as has been noted. And the schism between Eastern and Western Christendom was made more permanent. In addition, the Christian mission to Moslems, hard enough at best, was made immeasurably more difficult by the bitter enmities which the Crusades engendered between adherents of these two faiths. The dissolute lives of Crusaders in Palestine further confirmed the Moslem in his conviction that his faith was superior to Christianity.

3. *Christians Under Moslem Rule*

Spain was won back by Christians by a slow process culminating in 1492. However, a vast stretch of territory formerly Christian—at least nominally—remained in Moslem hands. Indeed, many of the great centers of early Christianity in North Africa, Egypt, Palestine, and Asia Minor were included. How did Christians fare under Islamic rule?

In the heat of conquest there was much destruction of churches and temples, with some forced conversion. However, although they ruthlessly suppressed paganism, the Moslems usually tolerated Christians and Jews as "people of the Book," people who had a revelation related to that of Moslems, though inferior. Christians might retain their religion, but they were subject to a special tax. They were in the status of subject peoples, or little states within the Moslem states.

Various regulations were imposed upon Christians. One of the most devastating was the law against converting a Moslem to Christianity. The other side of the coin was the absolute prohibition against the Moslem's accepting Christianity. In both cases the death penalty was imposed. In such a situation evangelistic growth was obviously impossible—if every convert were executed! So, Christian churches in Moslem states gradually died out or else survived as little defensive minorities turned inward upon themselves.

4. *Sectarian Divisions and Orthodoxy*

Since early times Islam has suffered schism and sectarian division, though it has also retained a remarkable degree of unity. The most serious division was that of the *Shia* or *Shiites* who dissented from the recognized succession of leadership. The Shiites contended that the true successor to Mohammed was not his kinsman Abu Bakr, the recognized caliph, but Ali, the cousin and son-in-law of Mohammed. The Shiites are themselves divided and exist today, about 25,000,-000 in number, chiefly in Iran and Iraq and to the east. The non-Shiite or orthodox Moslems are known as *Sunnis*, or followers of the *Sunnah*, and, of course, comprise the vast majority.

In addition, there are mystics or *Sufis*, with a type of religion similar to mysticism as found elsewhere. They cut across the divisions mentioned above and are not generally considered a separate division, though in some cases they have their own religious orders.

IV. THE FAITH AND CONDUCT OF THE MOSLEM

Beliefs and regulations by which the Moslem life is ordered have their authority in the Koran. The Moslem must believe certain dogmas. From these beliefs stems a code of laws to regulate the relations of man and God and man and man. The Moslem therefore sees belief and practice as a unity, with primacy given to belief.

1. *Fundamental Beliefs*

The faith of the Moslem includes six fundamental beliefs. They are: (1) Belief in God (Allah). (2) Belief in predestination. (3) Belief in angels, the messengers of Allah. (4) Belief in the prophets or apostles. (5) Belief in the Koran. (6) Belief in the day of judgment and the other world.

(1) *Belief in Allah* is the fundamental faith of the Moslem. The "Word of Witness" which he repeats again and again is: "I witness that there is no God but Allah and that Mohammed is his Prophet." This is an uncompromising monotheism confessing that God is one; a zealous unitarianism proclaiming that God is undivided, having no partner or associate to share his being. All polytheism or worship of many gods, is excluded. And this means the exclusion not only of Arabian idolatry but also of the Christian Trinity. Moslems consider Christians polytheists because they say, according to the Koran, "God is the third of three." The supreme sin is "associating" something with God. Nothing whatsoever is to be associated with God as sharing his Godhead or Godness, not even Christ and the Holy Spirit.

The character of Allah is expressed by the Moslem in ninety-nine "Beautiful Names," most of which come directly from the Koran. The Moslem rosary has a bead representing each of the "beautiful names." The use of the rosary helps to recall these names. The most important names for God are "The Compassionate" and "the Merciful."

In Moslem beliefs God is absolutely different from man. His revelation is actually a disclosure of his will rather than his nature. In his essential Being he remains unknown. Unlike the New Testament, the Koran does not teach that "God is love."

"What gives unity to all God's dealings is that He wills them all. . . . His will of itself is inscrutable. One may not, therefore, say that God is necessarily loving, holy, righteous, clement, or relenting, in every and all relations." [1]

(2) *Belief in predestination.*—This revelation of God as absolute sovereign over all gives rise to what is called the doctrine of predestination in Islam. Everything is attributed to the divine will. Although a measure of human freedom is also recognized in the Koran, the problem of sovereign divine will and human responsibility is not solved. In fact it is not Moslem but non-Moslem scholars who view this as a problem. John B. Noss sees a development in the Koran by which Allah becomes "less Jewish and more Arabian," and therefore more and more despotic.[2] Godfrey E. Phillips says that in Islam "man has no heavenly Father but a heavenly Sultan, and must behave accordingly." [3]

(3) *Belief in angels* is also essential to Moslem faith. Associated with it is belief in *jinn* and the soul. If God is absolutely different from man, then some being between God and man is necessary to bear God's message to man. This is an important function performed by angels. They are supernatural creatures which, of course, do not share in divinity. They are like men in character, but without shortcomings—except that there is a fallen angel who is the devil (*Iblis*).

Jinn are desert spirits, predominantly evil and thus demons, retained from Arabian pre-Islamic religion. They, too, are supernatural creatures but are of a lower order than the angels. Many of them tempt men to evil.

In the Koran several references are made concerning the soul or spirit, but there is little said about its nature. It is taught, however, that the soul continues to exist after death, either in bliss or in torment.

(4) *Belief in prophets or apostles* is another fundamental article of Moslem faith. Mohammed is the chief prophet. The prophets or apostles are ordinary men who have been chosen of Allah to receive his revelation as mediated through angels and proclaim it to mankind. The divine selection of the prophets guarantees the truth of their message. There are many prophets or apostles, including Noah, Abraham, Moses, and Jesus, and all of these must be believed. But Mohammed is the greatest prophet of all. He is called the "Seal of the Prophets" because God's revelation to all preceding prophets or apostles was incomplete and is now given complete and final, to Mohammed. Thus the second part of the Word of Witness: "I witness that there is no God but Allah and that *Mohammed is his Prophet*." Mohammed is accorded the highest honor and respect, but he is still human; he is not deified.

(5) *Belief in the scriptures* is the fifth basic belief of the Moslems. As Mohammed is the final Apostle, so the Koran is the final and complete scripture which includes and supercedes all previous scriptures. As Christians believe that Christ existed from all eternity, so Moslems believe that the Koran is eternally inscribed in heaven. To the Moslem, the Koran contains its own proofs of its divine origin and is "THE Miracle" of Islam.[4] The foundation of Islam is not "The Word become flesh." It is "The Word become book."[5]

(6) *Belief in the last day,* the resurrection and judgment day and the other world, is also part of Moslem belief. The penalty of disbelievers is the fire of hell. The reward of the righteous is the eternal blessedness of paradise. This blessedness is described quite sensuously: the blessed ones will recline on lined couches in pleasant gardens, with delightful

food and drink, with immortal youths to wait upon them, and with newly created virgins of surpassing beauty to be their companions.[6]

These, then, are the beliefs, or "facts," which every Moslem is expected to cherish. "Anyone who denies one of these Muslim facts cannot be treated as a Muslim nor subjected to the Muslim rules." [7]

2. *The Code of Conduct*

The code regulates the Moslem's relations to God and to his fellowman. The former comes under the heading of "worship of God" and is often called "The Five Pillars of Islam." The latter comes under the category of "dealings" with one's fellowmen.

(1) *Worship of God.*

The worship of God includes recitation of the Creed, prayer, fasting, payment of the religious tax, and pilgrimage.

a. The recitation of the Creed of Islam is the first step in becoming a Moslem. This Creed is called the "Word of Witness." It states: "I witness that there is no God but Allah, and that Mohammed is his Prophet." Its sincere repetition is the basic requirement of Islam.

b. Prayer.—The devout Moslem prays five times daily: in the early morning, at midday, in midafternoon, in the evening, and in the late evening. These prayers include repeating the name of the Lord, especially the statement of praise, "God is most great," and declarations of submission to God's will. They also involve kneeling a certain number of times with the forehead touching the floor (or prayer mat). The Moslem can perform his prayers anywhere: at home, at work, or at the Moslem house of worship, the *mosque.*

If the Moslem is in the proximity of the mosque, he will be reminded of the time of prayer by the call issued by the *muezzin* from the minaret, a tower attached to the mosque. The prayer call is as follows, except that each sentence is repeated: "God is most great. . . . I bear witness that there is no God but Allah. . . . I bear witness that Mohammed is the Apostle of God. . . . Welcome prayer. . . . Welcome good fortune. . . . God is most great. . . . There is no God but Allah."

On Friday there is a special weekly congregational service held at noon in the mosque's paved courtyard. If women are present, they ordinarily remain behind screens, unseen.

The men assemble at the call from the minaret. They go to the pool or fountain for their ceremonial washing of hands, mouth, nostrils, face, forearms, neck, and feet. Then they remove shoes and sit for a few minutes to hear a "reader," (*qari*) recite from the Koran. When the *imam,* or prayer leader, arrives, the worshipers arrange themselves in rows. They allow enough space to prostrate themselves in prayer. "During the ritual prayer (or *salat*) the *imam* recites all the necessary words and the worshippers silently and as one follow him in his motions. . . . After the prayer the *imam* usually preaches a sermon having as its purpose the exposition of Moslem doctrines." [8]

c. Fasting is the third aspect of Moslem worship. This religion expects its adherents to live in the daily routine of other men. However, for the month of *Ramadan* in the Moslem calendar, the Moslem fasts to commemorate the beginning of God's revelations to Mohammed in this same month. During Ramadan, the Moslem refrains from food, drink, and sexual intercourse from early dawn until sunset each day. One could imagine that in a hot, desert climate, the refusal of drink might become excruciating. It is expected that the Moslem will sample enough of starvation "to make him a warm-hearted, hospitable person, sympathetic with the poor who are in constant want." [9]

d. The religious tax, or zakat, is a provision by which the needs of the poor are met, and mosques, hospitals, schools, defense forces, and such are maintained. It prescribes percentages of income to be given, depending, for example, upon whether a farmer's land is watered by rain or irrigated. It was once required by national laws in Moslem lands but is now often voluntary. Even so, it is strongly expected that the Moslem will pay it.

e. The pilgrimage to Mecca, Islam's holiest spot, is an act of worship expected of every Moslem man or woman once during a lifetime, unless impossible. The ceremonies and festival at Mecca and its vicinity, during the sacred month of Mohammed's Hegira or flight from Mecca, is a kind of symbol of the universal brotherhood of Moslems and their full equality. For these ceremonies at Mecca, all Moslems, great and small, rich and poor, are required to wear similar white robes and thus to be shorn of class distinctions.

(2) *Dealings, or Conduct in Community*

In Islam no distinction is made between the sacred and secular. All of life is to be ordered by the will of Allah as expressed in the Koran and the *Sunnah,* the prophetic teachings outside the Koran which comprise the "derived law." Thus it is assumed that the government of a Moslem country will enact and enforce Islamic law.

There is space here for no more than the barest summary of Moslem requirements for moral living. There are prohibitions against murder, adultery, lying, drinking wine, and gambling. There are dietary regulations similar to those of the Old Testament. Family morality includes respect and kindness to parents, kindness to children and provision for their needs, and fidelity of the marriage partners. It is permissible for a man to have as many as four wives, but only if he can treat them equitably. Women are in an obviously inferior position, yet their status is elevated considerably over that which obtained in pre-Islamic Arabic society. Concern is shown and provision made for orphans, widows, and other needy members of society. Virtues of courage, moderation, perseverance, strength, and hospitality are emphasized.

The life of the Moslem, then, is regulated by Islamic law in terms of a morality which is in the reach of all.

V. CONTEMPORARY ISLAM

Islam is changing. As other religions it has always been subject to change and development. But change has been unusually difficult for Islam because of its rigid dogmatism. Now, however, as never before it is facing revolutionary influences.

1. *Factors Producing Change*

The world of Islam is becoming modernized. Prominent in the influences playing upon it are the universal sweep of secularism and the growth of a secular spirit. The ancient patterns of life, which have held tightly, especially in the Near East, are broken by the modern business and industrial world. Little time is left for devotional practices, and a premium is placed upon material values.

Moreover, Western education has entered the world of Islam, especially through Christian missions. Other contacts with the West have come about by Moslems' travel and education abroad. The creation of the State of Israel as a Western island in the Moslem world is also having its effect. The emergence of nation states in the Moslem areas, free from Western colonial domination, has nurtured nationalism which sometimes favors Islam and sometimes competes with it. By these factors and many others the modern world is influencing Islam.

2. *Reactions to Modern Influences*

In a book published in 1933, Charles S. Braden indicated four main types of reaction to the modern influences affecting Islam: indifferent, radical, liberal, and fundamental reactions.[10] These same types of reaction have continued. Perhaps indifference, though less conspicuous, is the most prevalent.

Indifference leads to the abandonment of Islam, especially as a system of government and law for the ordering of the state. It usually means also the adoption of an agnostic, humanistic, or atheistic attitude toward religion. This spirit is found throughout the Moslem countries, but it has been most apparent in Turkey. This country took the drastic step in 1924 of abolishing the *Caliphate*, the seat of Islamic religious leadership in succession to Mohammed. It followed this step with separation of religion and state. Friday, the Moslem holy day, was abandoned for Sunday, and the Moslem calendar was replaced by the Gregorian. Thus Turkey began to show itself as a secular rather than a Moslem state. And the spirit of secularism has spread widely.

In distinction from abandonment of Islam, there are many liberals who wish to adjust Islam to modern conditions and modes of thought. Though this group is composed largely of lay people, it is also participated in by some recognized teachers of Islam. Often the liberals advocate a return to original Islam and thus the riddance of many outmoded social regulations that have developed by tradition. Sometimes the liberals go so far as to welcome friendly intercourse with other religions and to apply modern critical methods to the study of the Koran. The effect both of radical and liberal tendencies has been social reform, for example, the elevation of the status of women in most Moslem lands.

There are also fundamentalist reactions which resist any change from traditional Islam. The *Wahhabi* movement antedates the modern period, having originated in the eighteenth century, but it has been extremely puritanical and conservative, insisting upon a return to the simplicity of original Islam. As such it has helped, on the one hand, to encourage some liberalizing reforms and, on the other, to foster a reactionary spirit. Its main purpose was to oppose innovations. There is also the *Salafi* movement, which insists upon traditionalism and a literal interpretation of the Koran. The spirit of orthodoxy is very prominent.

3. *Missionary Revival*

Another reaction to the modern situation is a resurgence of Moslem missionary spirit. Missionary expansion of Islam in the past has been largely an unorganized movement. It accompanied military expansion at first and commercial enterprises and emigration in later centuries. In the last three or four decades, however, a new type of missionary effort has developed. Trained missionaries are now sent in organized fashion. By the 1930's missionaries had been sent from India to China and from the Dutch East Indies to South Africa. An International Moslem Association for the propagation of Islam in the Far East had been formed, and an extensive home missionary enterprise was underway in India. In addition, a heretical sect of Islam called *Ahmadiyyah* was maintaining missions in a number of countries, including England and the United States.[11]

These missionary efforts have increased since World War II. The Ahmadiyya now operates as an independent missionary society in more than twenty countries. Islamic mosques and information centers may be found in many American and other Western cities, including the impressive one in Washington, D. C. The construction of that mosque was sponsored by sixteen Moslem nations.

In October, 1952, a Moslem congress was held in Indonesia. There, an organized movement known as "Missionary Islam," became evident. Its primary concern was to overcome all barriers to Moslem expansion.[12]

President Nasser of Egypt has encouraged the spread of Islam, especially in Africa, and has given his support to gathering funds for missionary work. Several hundred Moslem missionaries have been sent into Africa, where allegedly Islam is spreading faster than Christianity. The Moslem missionaries claim that Christianity preaches the doctrine of racial brotherhood but that Moslems both *preach* and *practice* it.

4. *The Black Muslims*

Mention must be made of what are called the "Black Muslims" or "Black Islam," even though they are not yet accepted within the pale of official Islam. Their importance is that they represent a unique American phenomenon of racism in reverse. They have reacted against discrimination toward the Negro and have replaced the myth of white supremacy with the opposite myth of black supremacy.

The movement originated in Detroit in the 1930's with a Negro who went by the name of W. D. Fard and also called himself Mr. Farrad Muhammad. His origins are still obscure and his disappearance in 1934 is also an unsolved mystery. The cult which he began is now headed by one of Fard's associates, Elijah Poole, a native of Georgia. Poole goes by the name Elijah Muhammad and is considered the messenger or apostle of the Black Muslims, while Fard is deified as Allah come to earth.

The movement is strongly pro-black man and preaches the doctrine of a Black Nation within America. The black man (including all nonwhites) is considered divine and the white man demonic. Christianity is strongly opposed because it is considered the religion of the white man. Prayer requirements are similar to those of Islam, as are dietary regulations. Tobacco is forbidden, and overeating is frowned upon. Strict sexual morality is enforced. Many criminals and social delinquents, such as prostitutes and drug addicts, have been reclaimed by Black Islam. Attendance at temple services (usually twice a week) is required, as is also the giving of a high percentage of a member's income to the movement.

The movement is growing rapidly and now numbers well over 100,000 adherents. In December, 1960, it was reported to have sixty-nine temples or missions in twenty-seven states.

FOR CLASS DISCUSSION

1. How did Islam originate?
2. What are the basic beliefs of Islam?
3. Discuss the missionary movement of modern Islam.
4. Describe the "Black Muslims." What should be the Christian attitude toward them?

NOTES

[1] Kenneth Cragg, *The Call of the Minaret* (New York: Oxford University Press, 1956), p. 42. Used by permission of Oxford University Press.

[2] Noss, *Man's Religions*, p. 699.

[3] Godfrey E. Phillips, *The Religions of the World* (Wallington, Surrey, England: The Religious Education Press, Ltd., 1948), p. 125. Used by permission of The Religious Education Press.

[4] Mohammed Abd Allah Draz, "The Origin of Islam," *Islam—the Straight Path*—Islam Interpreted by Muslims, ed. Kenneth W. Morgan (New York: The Ronald Press Company, 1958), p. 16. Used by permission of The Ronald Press Company.

[5] Hendrik Kraemer, *The Christian Message in a Non-Christian World* (New York: Harper and Brothers, 1938), pp. 217–218. Used by permission of Division of World Mission and Evangelism, The World Council of Churches.

[6] The Koran, LVI.

[7] Mahmud Shaltout, "Islamic Beliefs and Code of Laws," *Islam—the Straight Path*, ed. Morgan, p. 92.

[8] Noss, *op. cit.*, pp. 703–704.

[9] Shaltout, *op. cit.*, p. 116.

[10] Charles S. Braden, *Modern Tendencies in World Religions* (London: George Allen and Unwin, Ltd., 1933), pp. 191 ff.

[11] *Ibid.*, pp. 224 ff.

[12] Manikam, ed., *Christianity and the Asian Revolution*, p. 164.

SOME OTHER LIVING RELIGIONS

I. SHINTO: PRIMITIVE RELIGION IN A MODERN NATION
   1. Early Shinto
   2. Shinto Carried into the Modern World
   3. The Status of Shinto Today

II. PARSEEISM: VESTIGES OF A ONCE GREAT RELIGION
   1. Distribution and Statistics
   2. Zoroaster and the Beginnings of Zoroastrianism
   3. From Zoroaster to Present Parseeism

III. JAINISM: AN ANCIENT HINDU PROTESTANTISM
   1. The Founder
   2. The Basic Ideas of Jainism
   3. Present Status

IV. SIKHISM: AN ATTEMPT AT SYNTHESIS
   1. Background
   2. Origin and Development
   3. The Synthesis of Islam and Hinduism
   4. The Present Situation

V. BAHA'ISM: A NEW PROPHET AND A NEW SYNCRETISM
   1. Origin and Development
   2. Teachings of Baha'ism
   3. Methods of Propagation

8

Some Other Living Religions

THERE ARE religions other than the ones already discussed that, because of their small membership or geographical or other limitations, can be given only brief attention in this study. Such are Shinto, which is confined to Japan and Japanese; Parseeism, a Near Eastern religion represented by small communities in Iran and India; two nonexpanding Indian religions, Jainism and Sikhism; and Baha'ism, a relatively new attempt at a world faith through syncretism, the union of beliefs from different religions.

I. SHINTO: PRIMITIVE RELIGION IN A MODERN NATION

Shinto, with an estimated membership of about 34,000,000, presents the phenomenon of a primitive religion existing in one of the most literate nations of the world.

1. *Early Shinto*

Shinto, meaning the "Way of the Gods," is the native religion of the Japanese. Although the beginnings of Japan and her religion are hidden beneath myth and obscurity, as nearly as we can tell, Shinto was originally a vague nature worship with the general elements of animism and polytheism. The interest in food production and fertility was dominant. So there were deities and rites related to food production: agricultural deities, a storm-god, harvest festivals, and the like.

The idea of god was extremely vague. Most anything could be a *kami* or god, and the line between humanity and divinity was very thin. Ancestor worship appears in early Shinto, but this may have been added by Chinese influence.

The approach to the gods was one of friendly intimacy. Fear, which is the usual accompaniment of animism, was not prominent. The one requirement for contact with deity was purification. Defilements were many, and cleansing rites were of great importance.

Places of worship were very simple, originally just roped-off places where food offerings could be made. Later they became unpainted, but clean, buildings inside a roped-off area, with a distinctive gate called *torii*.

2. Shinto Carried into the Modern World

This simple, primitive religion still exists in its essential character in the highly educated Japan of today. Perhaps there are two principal reasons for this puzzling fact.

In the first place, Shinto became associated with the alleged divine origins of the imperial family and the Japanese nation. What seems to have happened is that Shinto myths were developed to explain and justify the unification of Japan under one strong clan, the Yamato. At any rate, in the eighth century A.D., two supposedly historical chronicles were produced. These chronicles involved mythological accounts of the lineage of the emperor (the Yamato chieftain). He was represented as a direct descendant of the greatest deity, the sun-goddess. Also, the chronicles traced the origin of the Japanese islands and people from lesser deities.

In the second place, Buddhism entered Japan and, from about the sixth century A.D., became a prominent vehicle for the importation of the ancient and highly developed Chinese culture. About the beginning of the ninth century, "marriage" of Buddhism and Shinto was accomplished, which proved to be mutually beneficial. The Shinto deities were identified as the appearance in Japan of the divine personages of Mahayana Buddhism. This union of Shinto and Buddhism helped Japanese accept Buddhism and served to insure Shinto's continuance into modern times.

For a long time, Shinto was practically swallowed up in Buddhism. During the Tokugawa period (1600-1867), Buddhism was the official religion of Japan. The nationalism which attended and followed the revolution of 1868 resulted in the reassertion of Shinto and the disestablishment of Buddhism as the state religion. Beginning about 1870, Shinto was developed as a patriotic cult of reverence for the emperor and for the deities responsible for Japan's origins and development. Thus the government had a national cult for engendering patriotism and maintaining imperial prestige. And the militaristic leaders who finally plunged Japan into the tragic war of the 1930's and 1940's, found in this cult a ready-made instrument for their use.

3. The Status of Shinto Today

(1) What has just been discussed as the national cult of patriotism is *State* or *Shrine Shinto*. This had been declared distinct from Sectarian Shinto in 1882. In 1945, under the occupational government headed by General Douglas MacArthur, Shrine Shinto was disestablished and placed on the same footing as all religions. The new constitution provided for the separation of religion and government, and the emperor publicly denied his divinity.

Shrine Shinto continues, however, on the basis of voluntary support. Individual worshipers frequent the shrines, and various ceremonies are performed by the priests. There are some tendencies in the direction of the re-establishment of Shrine Shinto, but these have not succeeded.

(2) *Sectarian Shinto* consists of thirteen so-called Shinto sects, though actually various non-Shinto elements are included and, in some cases, predominate. These thirteen are subdivided into three "Pure Shinto Sects," two "Confucian Sects," three "Mountain Sects," two "Purification Sects," and

three "Sects of Peasant Origin." The last group have their own founders and are more sophisticated than the others. They are very active in educational and social welfare work and missionary propagation. The other sects tend to be quite primitive in nature.

(3) Mention may be made here of Japan's so-called new religions, some of which are growing rather phenomenally. These are sects that have come into being in fairly recent years, many of them since the Second World War. Several of them contain Shinto elements, but others are predominantly Buddhist in nature. Most of them are syncretistic because they combine elements of several religions. Typical emphases are faith healing, the attainment of happiness and prosperity, and the divine nature of man.

II. PARSEEISM: VESTIGES OF A ONCE GREAT RELIGION

"Parseeism" is the name usually given today to Zoroastrianism, the religion of ancient Persia founded by Zoroaster (or Zarathushtra).

1. *Distribution and Statistics*

The word "Parseeism" is derived from the name given to Persians (or Iranians) who fled to India when persecuted by Moslems. They were called "Parsees." Most of those who follow the religion of Zoroaster are now in India. Of a world total of about 130,000 there are about 110,000 in India, with about half of these in the city of Bombay alone, and about 5500 in Pakistan. In Iran, the land of their origin, there are not more than 20,000. These are called *Gabars*, a word of uncertain origin. A few others are scattered throughout other lands.

2. *Zoroaster and the Beginnings of Zoroastrianism*

While Zoroaster is accepted as a historical personage, his birthplace and the dates of his life are uncertain. Information concerning him is fragmentary and unreliable. The traditional dates are 660-583 B.C., but he may have lived much earlier.

The accounts of Zoroaster's life somewhat parallel Buddha's experiences, though their beliefs were very dissimilar. There is the forsaking of home and wife, the period of searching and solitude, and eventual enlightenment.

Unlike Gautama, however, his enlightenment was in terms of a divine revelation of the one God, *Ahura Mazda*. Then ensued a discouraging period of several years of preaching, during which he suffered persecution and imprisonment. Finally, he won his king, Vishtaspa. Other converts followed, and the faith of Zoroaster was planted firmly in Iran. Meantime, the new religion had to be defended against the fierce Turanian invaders, one of whom murdered Zoroaster as he officiated at worship before the fire altar.

Zoroaster's message was a proclamation of the one Lord, *Ahura Mazda*, a term meaning something like "Lord Creator." This one God expresses his will through a Holy Spirit and the "Immortal Holy Ones," which seem to be personalized modes of Ahura Mazda's activity and revelation. This allows for a richness of the understanding of deity without the loss of monotheism. The symbol of Ahura Mazda is fire, and worship was simple rites at the fire altar.

Both good and evil are created by Ahura Mazda.[1] Thus the possibility of real good is provided by the struggle with evil. But evil, represented by the Bad Spirit, will ultimately be defeated. Each man has freedom to choose good or evil, falsity or truth. The human heart is the battleground between these two forces. Those who choose good are truthful. They work for the welfare of society by making the ground produce and by treating kindly the cow upon which life depends.

By contrast, those who choose evil destroy the crops and slay cattle, as do especially the wicked Turanians. (Here is seen a cultural struggle between those representing civilization—a settled life—and the barbarian nomads.) At the end, there is to be a general resurrection and a judgment which, by the test of ordeal, determines who is good and who is evil. And these enter either into heaven or hell.

3. *From Zoroaster to Present Parseeism*

The centuries following the death of Zoroaster brought undesirable changes to the religion he had founded. His monotheistic faith was compromised by the tendency to deify and worship Zoroaster himself and by the return of old Aryan gods in the form of angels and other beings that Zoroaster had recognized as creatures of God. These now became deities, and monotheism reverted to polytheism.

In addition, Zoroaster's concept of good and evil powers was developed until the Bad Spirit became practically co-equal and coeternal with the Lord Ahura Mazda, and the ultimate victory of good over evil became obscured. These internal changes were accompanied by external difficulties. Consequently, Zoroastrianism gradually dwindled, especially yielding ground to Islam, until it almost became extinct.

The present Parsees in India are conspicuous by their prominence in business and philanthropy, as well as by the distinctive headdress, resembling a bishop's miter, which the men wear. They have been unusually open to Western influences, and they are quite progressive and are held in high respect.

They still maintain their fire-temples, usually unpretentious buildings in which the fire, symbol of deity, is kept burning. In one of the Indian temples, the sacred fire has been burning, it is said, for well over one thousand years. Certain ceremonies, such as initiation, are also maintained; and scriptures, the *Avesta*, are preserved and revered.

Of special interest are the *dakhmas*, or "towers of silence." These are circular structures of brick or stone, located on hilltops, which afford funeral places. The corpse is placed on a floor within the structure, on a different level depending upon whether the dead person was a man, woman, or child. Vultures then come and dispose of the flesh; and, after the sunshine and wind bleach the bones, they are thrown into a central pit where they return to the dust. Thus the elements are kept undefiled by decaying flesh.

There are "modernist" Parsees who seek to reform their ancient religion and restore it to its original purity. Others have become secularized and have reacted against religion. Still others are conservative and resist both of these alternatives. Altogether, they represent remnants of a once noble faith which rose far above the primitive polytheism of its time and place.

III. JAINISM: AN ANCIENT HINDU PROTESTANTISM

Like Buddhism, Jainism originated as a protest or heresy in the developing organism of Hinduism. Both of these religions seem to have reacted against caste divisions, especially the dominance of the priestly (Brahman) caste—though caste later returned in Jainism. Also, both rejected the religion of the Vedas (the early Hindu scriptures), with its philosophical tendencies. However, they betray their essential Hindu character by retaining the doctrine of cause and effect (*karma*) and by viewing life's central problem as involvement in the endless chain of rebirths.

The word "Jain" is derived from *jina*, meaning "victor." The Jains number about 1,500,000 in India, a relatively self-enclosed religious community. Their temples, expressions of Indian art at its best, are among the most beautiful in the world.

1. *The Founder*

Nataputta Vardhamana, the founder of Jainism, was a native of Bihar, India. If one accepts the traditional dates for his life, 599-527 B.C., he was an older contemporary of Gautama. He is better known by his title, "Mahavira," which means "Great Man." Perhaps it is not literally correct to call him the founder of Jainism, because there are traditions that he was the last in a succession of religious leaders called *Tirthankaras,* or "ford-finders." Almost certainly there were groups of monks before and during his time who shared his general viewpoint.

The accounts of his life reveal the familiar pattern of restlessness and dissatisfaction concerning enlightenment and salvation, the forsaking of home and family, the period of quest, and finally enlightenment, followed by preaching and gathering disciples. Unlike Gautama, however, he found the answer to his search through extreme asceticism, or self-mortification. The scriptures of Jainism relate how he fasted, how he exposed his body to the cold of winter without clothing or shelter and to the heat of summer without shade. The scriptures tell how he sat unmoved when taunting villagers hissed dogs upon him or built a fire between his feet!

2. The Basic Ideas of Jainism

(1) The underlying assumption of this religion seems to be that of *animation*—all nature possesses life or the possibility of being animated. This is the basic feeling of primitive religion, but here it is set in a philosophical context.

(2) The Jains believe in *ahimsa,* "noninjury," the law of refraining from hurting any living being. To the Jain, this is the most essential ethical requirement.

(3) Another important idea is the twofold nature of reality: *jiva,* or souls, living beings, and *a-jiva,* or lifeless things. Both of these realities, souls and lifeless elements, are eternal.

(4) *Karma* is more than a law of cause and effect. It is a kind of matter which attaches itself to the soul.

(5) Many sins are listed, such as the taking of life, conceit, greed, hypocrisy, and others. Certain of these are divided

into degrees of indulgence. The insight here is that sin is worsened through one's clinging to it.

(6) *Asceticism,* the practice of self-torture and self-denial to attain a high spiritual state, is the surest and best means of salvation. Like Buddhism, Jainism provided for monks and nuns and lay orders. Monks were required to take five vows, and laymen a longer but more lenient list of twelve. The five vows of the monk are noninjury to living beings, truth-speaking, no stealing, sexual abstinence, and non-attachment.

The first of these vows, noninjury, creates difficulties—particularly if one knows about microbes in drinking water! The last is the most stringent of all: one is to allow himself to become attached to nothing and nobody.

Following this rigorous method will counteract bad *karma* with good and lead to liberation, and eternal bliss. This is self-salvation. No deities whatever are recognized—unless it is the essential divinity of a "Jain" or victor in the struggle for salvation. He presumably will exist eternally and with his separate identity.

3. *Present Status*

The avoidance of injury to living creatures has steered the Jains away from such occupations as agriculture, butchering, and fishing. The result is that the people have gravitated to more lucrative careers in banking, merchandising, real estate, and the professions. Therefore, though it seems contradictory, an extremely world-denying group has become rather wealthy. Also, their stringent morality has earned them social respect. Both of these factors have helped preserve them in spite of periods of persecution.

The Jains are divided into two main sects. The *Digambaras,* or "sky-clad," are very strict. They get their name from their insistence on nudity, clothing themselves only with the sky or atmosphere! They exclude women from their temples and permit no nunneries, holding to Mahavira's alleged judgment that women are the world's greatest source of temptation and sin.

The *Shvetambaras*, or "white-clad," are more liberal, permitting the wearing of at least one garment. They believe that women have the possibility of *Nirvana* without rebirth as a man, and they provide nunneries. In other ways they show themselves more liberal than the "sky-clad."

A smaller sect believes in no temples or images.

Having stagnated for centuries in formalism and ritualism, Jainism has for the past several decades manifested new vitality. An All-India Jain Association was founded in 1895, and other societies have sprung up, such as Jain Sacred Text Societies and Young Men's Jain Associations. Periodicals and books, also, are published, and the Jains are showing interest in propagating their faith in India and elsewhere.

IV. SIKHISM: AN ATTEMPT AT SYNTHESIS

Sikhism is the most recent religion to spring forth from the fertile soil of India. It began about A.D. 1500, in the same period as the Protestant Reformation. It is a syncretism, combining elements of Islam and Hinduism. As such it succeeded in merging elements of these two religions into one, but not in uniting the two religions themselves.

"Sikh" means "disciple" or "learner." And, although we call this religion "Sikhism," the Sikhs call it the religion of *Sat Nam*, the "True Name." Sikhs number about 6,000,000 in India today.

1. *Background*

The Moslem conquest of North India had brought Islam face to face with Hinduism and Buddhism. The effect upon Islam was the encouragement of mysticism. This Moslem mysticism, called *Sufism*, emphasized knowing God through the inner experiences of the soul. Conversely, the monotheism of Islam, belief in one God, influenced Hinduism toward the development of Bhakti, devotion to one deity, which tended toward monotheism. The consequence was a drawing together of the two religions, at least in the minds of some of the adherents of both. From the twelfth century to the beginning of Sikhism, there were several religious leaders who were influenced by Sufi-Islam and Bhakti-Hinduism.

2. Origin and Development

Nanak (1469-1538), the founder of Sikhism, was the culmination of this development. He was of the Jat racial group, a lower bracket of the warrior or Kshatriya caste, a native of northwest India, and a Bhakti Hindu. After an early marriage, he encountered domestic troubles. Consequently, following the birth of his second child, he left home, disappearing in the forest.

Already mystically inclined, Nanak now had a vision of God's presence in which he was instructed to go and repeat God's name and cause others to do so. Shortly thereafter, he emerged from the forest. After a day of silence, he announced that there is no Hindu and no Moslem, meaning that these two are essentially the same.

Nanak preached and gained converts, and thus a new religious movement was born. Before Nanak died, he appointed a successor and announced that this new *guru* (teacher) had inherited the divine spirit which was in him. Then followed two hundred years of history and a succession of ten *gurus.*

Meanwhile, under Moslem persecution, the Sikhs exchanged an early pacifism for increasing militarism. The tenth *guru,* Govind Singh (1675-1708), welded his followers into a military as well as religious brotherhood and began the practice of a "sword baptism," by which the Sikhs were sprinkled with sweetened water which had been stirred with a sword. One thus baptized was called a *Singh,* or "lion."

Govind also ordained for his followers five distinguishing marks, called the five K's. These were: the *Kangha,* a steel comb to be worn in the hair; the *Kes,* long hair and beard; the *Khanda,* a steel sword; the *Kara,* a steel bracelet; and the *Kackh* or short drawers (from which comes the word "khaki"). The first two of these are still adhered to by devout Sikhs.

Another innovation of Govind was the termination of the line of human *gurus* (teachers). He proclaimed that the Sikh scripture, the Adi Granth, was henceforth to be the only *guru.*

Before 1800 the Sikhs were able to carve out for themselves the territory called the Punjab as a kingdom. And, in spite of continued war with the Moslems, they succeeded in maintaining themselves until the British added the Punjab to their colonial empire in 1849. Thereafter they attained fame as soldiers in the British armies.

3. *The Synthesis of Islam and Hinduism*

From Islam, Sikhism adopted the doctrines of the sovereign transcendence and unity of God, predestination, equality of men, and opposition to idolatry. From Hinduism, it retained the law of cause and effect (*karma*), the doctrine of rebirth of souls, and *maya,* the unreality of the natural world. All of these may be found in the Sikh scripture. Obviously these diverse elements are not easily harmonized. Most important, however, was the concept of one personal God, who is ruler of the world but yet present in it.

The doctrine of salvation was neither distinctively Moslem nor Hindu. Man is to adore God by repetition of the True Name and glorify him by service to mankind. Ritual is entirely unnecessary. Many rebirths into the world may be involved before salvation occurs. Final salvation is absorption into God.

Sikhism, then, was a synthesis or blend of Moslem and Hindu elements, resulting in a new religion.

4. The Present Situation

Since the Sikhs are concentrated in one Indian state, Punjab, their political importance is out of proportion to their relatively small numbers. They are a sturdy, self-reliant people. Except for those who have become secularized, they continue their religious practices at their temples.

Recent writers on Sikhism tend to be pessimistic about its future as a religion. One of their own number published a book on the Sikhs in 1953, giving as his chief reason for writing the book the expectation that the Sikhs as a people will have become extinct by the end of the century. [2] The reasons for this pessimistic prediction are two: (1) the decline in observance of the forms and symbols of the faith and the consequent absorption into Hinduism; and (2) internal stress, jealousies, and conflicts caused by the development of caste-consciousness within the Sikh community.

V. BAHA'ISM: A NEW PROPHET AND A NEW SYNCRETISM

Out of Shiite Islam in Iran has come a new religion, Baha'ism, which is of special significance because it has a considerable following in the United States. The *Yearbook of American Churches*, edition for 1962, indicates that there are 229 local assemblies of Baha'i in continental United States and constituents in more than 1600 cities and towns.[3] The number of adherents is not indicated.

1. Origin and Development

The involved history of this movement can be summarized only very briefly here. It originated in Persia (Iran) in 1844, with the claim of a heretical Moslem, Mohammed Ali, to be the *Bab*, meaning the "Gate" or door to divine truth. Because of alleged political claims, he was put to death in 1850, as were also several of his followers. It is claimed, however, that before his death the *Bab* prophesied that an educator, greater than he, was coming, who would carry on his work and bring illumination and quickening to mankind.

Upon the death of the *Bab*, one of his followers, Mirza Hussain Ali, who had taken the name of Baha'ullah, meaning "Glory of God," assumed leadership. After imprisonment and exile to Baghdad, Baha'ullah declared himself to be the great one prophesied by *Bab*. Those who accepted this claim changed from "Babis" to "Baha'is," naming themselves after Baha'ullah.

The new prophet, unable to return to Persia, developed a center of the faith in Akka, Palestine. Baha'ullah was a very intelligent man, and he gave vigorous leadership to the movement until his death in 1892. He was then succeeded by his son, Abbas Effendi, who took the name of Abdul Baha, "Servant of Baha." Upon Abdul's death in 1921, his son, Shoghi Effendi, assumed leadership.

The movement is now organized into elective national assemblies and a world center at Haifa and Akka, Israel. The headquarters of the "National Spiritual Assembly" in the United States is at Wilmette, Illinois, a suburb of Chicago, where there is a remarkable Baha'i temple.

2. *Teachings of Baha'ism*

The character of this religion was determined by Baha'ullah, who is considered to be the great teacher and prophet whose message supercedes and fulfils all previous revelations. Therefore, the Baha'i movement seeks to unite all religions around Baha'ullah as the focal center.

The teachings of Baha'ullah were summarized by his son, Abdul Baha, in the following set of principles: (1) the oneness of the human race, (2) the independent investigation of truth, (3) the essential oneness of all religions, (4) the ideal of religious unity, (5) the accord of religion with science and reason, (6) the equality of men and women, (7) the abandonment of prejudices, (8) universal peace, (9) universal education, (10) solution of the economic problem, (11) a universal language, and (12) a world tribunal.[4]

Tracts published by the Baha'i Publishing Trust claim that the prophecies of Christianity, Judaism, Islam, Buddhism, Hinduism, and Zoroastrianism have been fulfilled in God's Messenger, Baha'ullah, who has begun a new, divine order, to which followers of all religions are now turning.

3. Methods of Propagation

In addition to personal witness of Baha'i believers and the dissemination of information from the assemblies, tracts and books are published and lectures are sponsored. The New History Society, founded in New York City in 1929, has sponsored such publications and lectures, and from this society has emerged a youth movement entitled "The Caravan of East and West." The Caravan has chapters in many countries and publishes periodicals about the movement.

Here, then, is a relatively new and ambitious attempt to syncretize the world religions, uniting them into one. We may expect that it will but add one more to the total.

FOR CLASS DISCUSSION

1. What is Shinto? What is Parseeism?
2. What are the basic doctrines of Jainism?
3. Did Sikhism succeed in blending Hinduism and Islam?
4. What are the main teachings of Baha'ism?

NOTES

[1] Irach J. S. Taraporewala, "Zoroastrianism," *Religion in the Twentieth Century*, ed. Ferm, p. 28.

[2] Khushwant Singh, *The Sikhs* (London: George Allen and Unwin, Ltd., 1953), p. 7.

[3] Benson Y. Landis, ed., *Yearbook of American Churches*, edition for 1962 (New York: National Council of Churches of Christ in the U.S.A., 1961), p. 16.

[4] Mirza Ahmad Sohrab, "The Bahai Cause," *Religion in the Twentieth Century*, ed., Ferm, p. 313.

THE CHRISTIAN REVELATION AND MAN'S RELIGIONS

I. THE PRESENT ENCOUNTER AND ITS MEANING FOR CHRISTIANS
   1. Being "Missionized"
   2. Our Religion Interpreted by Non-Christians
   3. Our Convictions of Religious Liberty Tested
   4. Challenged to Restudy Our Attitudes and Our Mission

II. CHRISTIANITY AND THE RELIGIONS: SOME DIFFERING INTERPRETATIONS
   1. "All Black and All White"
   2. All Religions Essentially One
   3. Revelation in Christ and General Revelation

III. THE CHRISTIAN ATTITUDE
   1. The "Golden Rule"
   2. "Radical Humility"
   3. "Downright Intrepidity"

The Christian Revelation
and Man's Religions

THIS STUDY has aimed at fairness in the presentation of the non-Christian religions. No attempt has been made to depreciate them or put them in a bad light. For the most part, the descriptions of their beliefs and practices have been drawn from the writings of adherents of these faiths themselves. A minimum of interpretation from the Christian standpoint has been injected.

In the discussion up until now, references have been made here and there to the challenge which these diverse convictions and "gospels" pose to the Christian faith and mission. The time has come, however, to focus attention upon the problem: What is the meaning of the present encounter of Christianity with the conflicting religious claims?

I. THE PRESENT ENCOUNTER AND ITS MEANING
FOR CHRISTIANS

1. *Being "Missionized"*

One meaning of the contemporary encounter of Christianity and non-Christian religions is that it is a two-way missionary street. For centuries Christianity has had a near monopoly of deliberately planned and organized missionary activity. But the situation is quite different today.

Christianity is the only religion which consistently, from its beginning until now, has made a universal claim and believed itself destined to become the world religion. It is, in fact, universal in the sense that it has proved itself religiously satisfying to people of all races and cultures. Some citizens of practically every country in the world today not only profess Christian faith but also participate in its further expansion. Other "missionary" religions depend in part upon Christianity for their present sense of mission—whether because of the example of Christianity or the desire to counteract its missionary success.[1]

But whatever the reason, there *is* new missionary zeal and activity on the part of non-Christian religions. This is especially true of Islam, Hinduism, and Buddhism, not to mention Baha'ism and other recently born missionary religions. *The truth is that for the first time so-called Christendom is being missionized.* We are no longer simply those who carry on missionary work. We are now the objects of missions. This missionary effort may be by direct non-Christian missionary propaganda or by the more subtle influences within our culture which would convert us to a non-Christian religious viewpoint while possibly leaving our church membership and participation undisturbed. That we are being missionized by non-Christian religions is a reality with which we must reckon. But there is more.

2. *Our Religion Interpreted by Non-Christians*

Until recently there have been two fairly characteristic reactions on the part of promoters of other religions in their encounter with Christianity. The first of these was the tendency, apparent for some time, of judging Christians and Christian countries by Christian standards. For example, a Buddhist might criticize American Christians upon the basis not of Buddhist but of *Christian* ethical standards.

The second reaction is the widespread copying of Christianity by non-Christian religionists. This copying is seen not only in the more superficial borrowings as shown in Buddhist Sunday schools, congregational worship services,

Y.M.B.A.'s and the like. It also includes a reinterpretation by the promoters of non-Christian religions of their beliefs and practices to make them resemble Christianity. Both of these tendencies pay Christianity a compliment. They amount to a tacit recognition of its superiority. [2]

Increasingly, however, with the end of Western dominance of the Eastern world and the revival of non-Christian cultures and religions, scholars of other faiths are studying and interpreting Christianity from the standpoint of their own religion. The inclination to accept Christian standards of judgment and to conform their religions to Christianity seems to be fading as this new propaganda develops.

An example is the attitude of the world-famous Japanese philosopher and Zen Buddhist, Dr. D. T. Suzuki. In a recent book,[3] Dr. Suzuki sees the cross as a symbol of the great psychological division between Buddhism and Christianity—between East and West.

He contrasts this gruesome crucifixion image with the picture of Buddha reclining on a bed surrounded by his disciples. The vertical stance of the cross symbolizes to Dr. Suzuki the "combative and exclusive" and "sometimes domineering" character of Christianity. On the other hand, the horizontal, reclining figure of the Buddha suggests "peace, tolerance, and broad-mindedness." [4] "The crucified Christ is a terrible sight," says Dr. Suzuki, "and I cannot help associating it with the sadistic impulse of a psychically affected brain." [5]

Likewise, the urbane and learned Hindu philosopher and statesman, Sir Sarvepalli Radhakrishnan, obviously tones down the uncompromising demand of the New Testament for decision concerning Christ.

He quotes with approval Jesus' words, "He that is not against us is for us" (Mark 9:40, RSV) as proof that "Jesus counts those who adopt other views but practice goodness, among His friends." [6] But he quite overlooks the fact that the man referred to was not one who chose to "practice goodness" apart from Christ but rather a man casting out demons in Jesus' name; and he conveniently ignores another statement of Jesus that "he that is not with me is against me" (Matt. 12:30).

Dr. Radhakrishnan defines the kingdom of heaven in Indian terms as "the state of enlightenment." He declares that "Christian teaching in its origin before it became organized and externalized was awakening from sleep through the light shed by the inner wisdom. Jesus, like the Buddha, was one who had awakened and taught others the way of awakening." [7]

This interpretation—and misinterpretation— of Christianity by the promoters of other religions is something to which we may as well get accustomed in the encounter of Christianity and non-Christian faiths today. Perhaps it will temper our impatience and irritation to recall that for a long time we Christians have explained—and misexplained—other religions from *our* perspective.

3. *Our Convictions of Religious Liberty Tested*

Almost certainly we shall see the increase of missionary activity and anti-Christian propaganda on the part of the other religions. And this within our own society which we like to think of as "Christian"—though actually it, too, is a mission field. To have non-Christian faiths propagated at our own doorsteps, accompanied by what appears to be a deliberate distortion of the meaning of Christianity, will put our convictions of religious freedom to a further test.

Again, it is helpful to remember that in our missionary work we have asked for and deeply cherished the right to propagate our faith in societies that are called "Buddhist" or "Moslem." We need to remember, also, that members of these societies have sometimes complained that their religions were being quite falsely interpreted by Christian missionaries. We must make sure that seeming threats to the status and security of our religion will not impel us to compromise our conviction of religious liberty. We believe in religious freedom even for those who deny our faith and try to convert us to some other religion.

Maybe the greater danger is that we succumb to some notion of tolerance which is not grounded in the gospel itself. Christian tolerance is not based on agnosticism, the idea that we really cannot know ultimate or final truth. Nor is it based on relativism, the notion that all religions are primarily cultural products, and that therefore none of them can claim any final revelation. Perhaps some popular varieties of tolerance in America today are based on these notions. But, from the perspective of Christian value judgment, they seem not only less but also lower than Christian tolerance.

The Christian's tolerance is that of one who believes that God *has* spoken a final word to all mankind in Jesus Christ, who is *the* way, *the* truth, and *the* life (John 14:6); and who yet defends not only the right of men to confess and propagate this faith but also their right to reject it and propagate a conflicting belief. This tolerance is based on the Christian understanding of God as the God of patient, seeking love, who never coerces but rather persuades, knocking at the door that men might *let* him in (Rev. 3:20). So tolerance is required by the nature of the gospel.[8]

4. *Challenged to Restudy Our Attitudes and Our Mission*

Especially does the new meeting of Christianity and other religions require that we give serious attention to the nature of the Christian mission in a non-Christian world. Christian theologians, as never before, are attempting this.

The theology of the Christian mission, particularly as it concerns the relationship of the Christian revelation to other claims to religious truth, is one of the very most vital issues in modern theology. A generation or so ago, Christian theologians could study and write in their field for a lifetime without any notice of the nature of the church's mission and the problem of relationship to other religions. This is hardly possible today.

It is doubtful if a contemporary theologian of reputation can be named who has not given some attention to these problems. The number of books on these subjects is steadily —and rapidly—growing. It is to be hoped that more and more, this kind of study and knowledge will become a part of the educational program of churches and will be the province of their membership in general and not confined to professional scholars and theologians.

II. CHRISTIANITY AND THE RELIGIONS: SOME DIFFERING INTERPRETATIONS

The relationship of Christianity to the religions is interpreted variously by Christian thinkers today.

1. *"All Black and All White"*

One interpretation is the sharpest kind of contrast. It is a simple case of "black and white." The other religions are thoroughly false and Christianity is thoroughly true. This is at best an uncritical opinion, but perhaps was the predominant view among Christians until the nineteenth century.

Certain factors of the modern world, however, including the modern missionary movement and the rise of the scientific study of religion have rendered this view obsolete. We may grant that pure Christianity is all true, though as it actually is taught and practiced, it certainly has its faults. But we must also admit that there are elements of truth and right in other religions. Even the brief introduction to the religions in the preceding chapters of this book confirms this fact. And our Christian theology must be able to recognize truth where-ever found or it is not a true theology.

2. *All Religions Essentially One*

The idea that all religions are essentially one is the view of Vedanta Hinduism and of Baha'ism. Interestingly, how-ever, both Vedanta and Baha'ism represent themselves as the religion into which all others are to merge, or the religion which includes and fulfils all others. This is actually a claim of the superiority of their own religions, or of their own in-sight or revelation—a claim which they condemn in other faiths!

However, our particular interest here is that this same view, namely, the essential oneness of all religions, is also held by many Christians. It was noticed at the end of chapter 3 that a prominent Asian Christian remarked that American popular religion is as pure a form of Vedanta as he had seen.

One meets this Vedanta idea on all sides. People often say, "All religions are essentially the same. One is as good as an-other, and no one should try to convert another person from one religion to another."

Once in a while a Christian layman will boldly express this idea, having secretly believed it for a long while. Popular books on world religions proclaim it, presumably as a pro-found Christian insight.[9]

However, there are not only laymen but also some very in-telligent Christian scholars who hold this view, though in a sophisticated form. Perhaps the best example is the world-renowned historian, Professor Arnold J. Toynbee.[10] Toynbee views the higher religions as varying expressions, in differing cultural environments, of the encounters of human beings with the one Absolute Reality which is present in, but also beyond, all historical events. In other words, to Toynbee, all religions are products of divine revelation. As such, they are variations on a single theme, the heavenly music of which, if heard simultaneously on earth, would be harmony rather than discord.

Toynbee points out that all of these higher religions are facing common problems and common foes. He says that the most fearful common enemy is collective man-worship, especially manifest in extreme nationalism and communism. He believes, also, that the religions must stand together against this formidable adversary by "preaching the supremely important negative belief" which they hold in common, namely "that man is not the highest spiritual presence in the universe." [11]

Toynbee claims that in this warfare, each religion has the urgent task of disengaging its essentials from its nonessentials. He even proposes that Christianity should get rid of the belief (which he admits is intrinsic to it) that it is unique.

Though Toynbee is too realistic to predict a syncretistic merger of religions, he hopes for their peaceful coexistence, with mutual reverence, admiration, and love.

Perhaps a commentary on Professor Toynbee's view will serve also as a brief analysis of this general viewpoint of the oneness of religion. Look again at his suggestion that Christianity slough off its Western (European and American) characteristics. Many Christian missionary statesmen have been urging this for a long time. They know that it is essential to effective Christian missionary expansion in the Eastern world. It is recognized, however, that this can only be done in relative measure and that, in any case, it is more easily said than done.

Undoubtedly, Christianity must always seek to distinguish between its essential nature and its cultural accessories, which may sometimes be excess baggage for its missionary pilgrimage. It is good to have this reminder from Professor Toynbee, though others have stated this requirement with more profound understanding of Christianity's nature.

As for Dr. Toynbee's proposal that Christianity purge itself of its claim to uniqueness, this is, in effect, asking Christianity to convert to another religion. For if Christianity ceases to hold to the unique revelation of God in the incarnate life, sacrificial death, and triumphant resurrection of Jesus Christ, it will have purged away its essential nature.

Two other comments need to be made: (1) The claim that the higher religions are one in essence simply cannot be squared with the facts. One can sustain this claim only by ignoring certain aspects of these religions and misrepresenting others for his own purposes. If all of Hinduism alone could be heard at once as "heavenly music," for example, would this be harmony or discord? And if you add to the orchestra Buddhism (which, after all, separated from Hinduism in protest), Islam, and Christianity, would you really hear harmony?

Can the doctrine of *karma* be made to mean the same as the Christian concept of sin and forgiveness? What about the Hindu goal of liberation—absorption into the impersonal World Soul? Is it just another expression of the Christian vision of redeemed persons living eternally with God in a society where reconciliation with God and man is complete, and righteousness and love are brought to perfection? Is the impersonal Brahman really identical with the God and Father of our Lord Jesus Christ? Is not the God of Islam a God who, by definition, cannot be incarnate? And is not the God of modern Judaism precisely the God who *did not* become flesh in Jesus Christ?

Some scholars of other faiths, even though their own religions deny the possibility of a final revelation, admit—at times unintentionally—that there are deep, irreconcilable differences between religions. D. T. Suzuki, the Buddhist scholar, sees a "gap which lies deep between Christianity and Buddhism." This difference is that, while Christianity insists upon the necessity of crucifying the self, "Buddhism declares that there is from the beginning no self to crucify. To think that there is the self is the start of all errors and evils." [12]

Dr. Radhakrishnan, the Hindu, while declaring the essential unity of all religions, yet condemns the Jewish and Christian doctrine of a chosen people. Christians would argue that, rightly understood, this doctrine is essential to Christianity.

(2) It must also be said that Toynbee's proposal that religions get together to combat collective man-worship in its horrible forms looks like the misuse of religion for human ends. Dr. Lesslie Newbigin is right when he says:

"If anything would qualify for being decorated with that overworked adjective *demonic*, it would be an alliance of religions to combat nationalism and communism. We have surely already enough evidence to show what happens when religion is used, I say used, for that kind of purpose. Christianity, at least, cannot submit to that treatment. . . .

". . . Such an alliance of the so-called higher religions of mankind, even if it were possible, would be the final form of man's self-worship. The only thing that can finally humble mankind is an act of God his creator. The Christian message is that God has performed such an act, an act of utter self-abasement for man's sake." [13]

The crux of the matter, then, is that Christians believe that God has acted uniquely and finally for man's redemption in Jesus Christ. To forsake this conviction of uniqueness is to abandon Christian faith.

3. Revelation in Christ and General Revelation

Most Christian theologians find some relationship between Christianity and other religions on the basis of a "general" or "original" revelation of God in nature and in human nature. This permits one to hold firmly to the belief in the uniqueness and finality of the revelation in Christ and at the same time recognize that God is at work in the whole world of human culture, including religion, not leaving himself without witness (Acts 14:17). "For what can be known about God is plain to them, because God has shown it to them. Ever since the creation of the world his invisible nature, namely, his eternal power and deity, has been clearly perceived in the things that have been made" (Rom. 1:19–20, RSV).

There are several variations of this general view, but three are suggested as representative.

(1) *Christianity as fulfilment* of what truth and revelation there are in other religions was a popular view among missionary theologians early in this century. A splendid example of this interpretation was a book by J. N. Farquhar, a scholarly missionary to India, entitled *The Crown of Hinduism*. In this book, published in 1913, Farquhar tried to show how the various strands of Hindu belief and practice come to their real fulfilment in Christ and the Christian religion.

From the perspective of modern theological scholarship, Farquhar's book, for all its fine Christian insight and learning, appears quite naive. It blurred the deep, unbridgeable differences between Hinduism and Christianity. More specifically, it failed to see that much of Hinduism would not be fulfilled, but destroyed and replaced when Hindus accepted Christian faith.

This points up the generally recognized fact that the concept of Christianity as fulfilment can be held today only in a qualified sense. Christ does fulfil such truth and revelation as are found elsewhere, but he also judges and condemns much that lies at the heart of man's religions. Where the central quest of a religion is to *get rid of* life, for example, Christ creates the new desire to *live* for the glory of God.

Moreover, these religions and their scriptures cannot replace the Old Testament as "tutors" or "custodians" to bring men to Christ (Gal. 3:23–25), because the biblical revelation is unique and unitary. Historically, the incarnate Christ did not come as a Messiah promised by the Vedas or some other non-Christian scripture. He came as the Messiah of the prophetic revelation of the Old Testament.

(2) *The "Logos" concept* is also employed today as a clue for understanding the relationship between the unique and final revelation in Christ and possible revelation elsewhere. This idea is based primarily upon the first chapter of John's Gospel. "In the beginning was the Word [Logos], and the Word was with God, and the Word was God. . . . And the Word became flesh and dwelt among us" (John 1:1, 14, RSV).

According to this interpretation, the *Logos* ("Word" or "Self-Expression") of God was eternally existing before he became incarnate as the full revelation of God. This eternal *Logos*, or Word of God, has been at work from the beginning, revealing God in his creation. He was "the true light which lighteth every man" (John 1:9); "He was in the world, and the world was made by him, and the world knew him not" (John 1:10).

Thus, one may expect to find at least fleeting glimpses of the revealing work of Christ, the eternal Word, even where the gospel has never been preached, though this previous revelation may be obscured and perverted. Those who have seen, even dimly, and cherished the light of the *Logos* may be expected to welcome the Light in its fulness when he appears (John 3:21).

(3) *"Discontinuity"* is an unwieldy term applied to the view that there is no organic relation between the Christian revelation and man's religions. According to this interpretation, the religions are impressive creations of man and products of the religious consciousness. Therefore, common elements of the religions, such as prayer and sacrifice, are not rooted in a common revelation but in the common religious consciousness in man. Standing over against human

religions in utter uniqueness and unrelatedness is the revelation of God in Christ.

Although there are values in the religions, *as religious systems* they are judged by the revelation in Christ as unbelief or sin. They shut men away from God. Therefore, the concept of the fulfilment of the other religions in Christ, as though there is some continuous line of development through them to him, is strongly denied.

Nevertheless, those who hold this view do not usually deny some kind of general or original revelation. They simply do not see it as important in determining the relationship of the Christian revelation and the religions. And they interpret it "dialectically," in terms of a yes and no. Hendrik Kraemer, the most noted proponent of this viewpoint, expresses its dialectic in terms of the story of Genesis 3:

"... the truth about man is that *he, in religious, moral and psychological respects, i.e., in his total being, finds himself through the Fall in an inescapably dialectical condition; related to God—separated from Him; sought by God ("Adam, where art thou" ...) and haunted by Him—rebelling against Him and yet groping towards Him.* This dialectical condition is the constitutive element of man's religious consciousness." [14]

This general position of discontinuity may be criticized as making a blanket judgment upon religions which is too harsh. Can Buddhism, Islam, Confucianism, and the other great religions be adequately described by the terms, "unbelief" or "sin"? A more fundamental criticism is that, although a strong case is made for the discontinuity between Christian revelation and non-Christian religion, no adequate account is given of the relationship between general or original revelation and the specific and ultimate revelation in Christ. For this purpose, the *Logos* concept might be effectively employed.

All three of these views make recognition of God's revealing activity in all his creation, a recognition which the biblical doctrine of God requires. But they also strongly affirm the missionary conviction which is of the essence of biblical faith. Whatever fleeting glimpses men have of the true Light in original revelation are at best but dim, flickering lamps with blackened globes. The darkness in which they faintly glimmer can be illumined only by the brilliant, warm "light of the knowledge of the glory of God in the face of Jesus Christ" (2 Cor. 4:6).

III. THE CHRISTIAN ATTITUDE

A concluding word needs to be said about the Christian attitude toward other religions. This has been implicit in much of our discussion, but it needs to be made explicit.

1. The "Golden Rule"

"And as ye would that men should do to you, do ye also to them likewise" (Luke 6:31). This Golden Rule indicates the Christian attitude. It means scrupulous fairness in our estimate of other religions. If it is unfair for a non-Christian to give a consciously biased interpretation of another religion, then it is certainly wrong for a Christian to do so. If it is wrong for a believer of a non-Christian religion to compare his religion at its best with ours at its worst, the reverse is also true, isn't it? And if we really have confidence in the uniqueness, finality, and utter superiority of the revelation of God in Christ, we do not need to be nervous about admitting the best in other religions.

2. "Radical Humility"

"I am made all things to all men, that I might by all means save some" (1 Cor. 9:22). In this fashion the apostle Paul expresses an essential missionary attitude of Christianity. He understood the role of the church and the Christian as servant of all men (1 Cor. 9:19). He based this understanding upon the example of Christ, who, though sharing in the sovereign glory of the eternal God, became a servant for our sakes. He shared our humanity, and endured our death. Thus he brings us to share in his risen life.

This means that the Christian, with the profoundest love and understanding, seeks to enter into the experience of the non-Christian in real identification and empathy.

Suppose a Moslem were to move to your community and engage you in conversation with the intent of converting you. If in the course of the conversation it became obvious that he knew nothing of your religion and did not care to know, what would you think? No doubt you would think him bigoted, dogmatic, and narrow-minded. But the judgment is the same if the situation is reversed.

This humble identification is an urgent necessity for missionaries who work in the world of non-Christian religions. They must be vitally interested in the religions of those to whom Christ sends them. This same understanding is increasingly imperative for all of us who are witnesses for Christ in a non-Christian world. Many of the world religions are quite ancient. They have profoundly influenced great cultures of Asia and the Near East by their lofty ethical teachings. Understandably, the members of these religions are proud. Attitudes of superiority and condescension on the part of American Christians deeply offend them.

Let us hold a firm conviction of the uniqueness and finality of Jesus Christ in a heart that loves and appreciates and sympathizes with all men in their religion or lack of it. We must become "all things to all men" for the sake of Christ and the gospel, and for the sake of the non-Christian.

3. *"Downright Intrepidity"*

". . . The attitude towards the non-Christian religions is a remarkable combination of downright intrepidity and of radical humility," [15] wrote the great missionary theologian,

Hendrik Kraemer. Radical humility, because church and Christian are only sharing a gift which is in no way their own achievement and which belongs to every man as much as to them. Radical humility, because our Lord took the form of a servant.

By "downright intrepidity," Kraemer meant uncompromising conviction and courage. The Christian witnesses without apology because he knows that his message is not his own discovery but God's act. The Christian knows that he is not and cannot be saved by his "religion," that is, by virtue of his moral and religious achievements. Therefore, in the face of the loftiest moral and religious achievements of the non-Christian religions, he declares boldly the message of salvation in Jesus Christ which brings conversion and regeneration.[16]

Christianity is different from all other religions, simply because it is the religion which the gospel produces and the religion which witnesses to the gospel. It is the religion of forgiven sinners who joyfully declare what wonderful things God has done for all men in Jesus Christ.

The gospel of God's free act of grace in Jesus Christ stands over against all of man's religions in uniqueness and finality. It addresses every man, in his religion or lack of religion, with the call to submit himself to this one Lord who proposes to redeem all of life and to make all things new.

FOR CLASS DISCUSSION

1. What is meant by the statement that "we are being missionized" by other religions?
2. What is "general revelation"?
3. What should be the Christian attitude toward other religions?

NOTES

[1] *Cf.* A. C. Bouquet, *The Christian Faith and Non-Christian Religions* (New York: Harper and Brothers, 1958), pp. 1–3.

[2] *Ibid.*, p. 9.

[3] Daisetz Teitaro Suzuki, *Mysticism: Christian and Buddhist* (New York: Harper and Brothers, 1957). Used by permission of Harper and Row, Publishers, Inc.

[4] *Ibid.*, pp. 137–138.

[5] *Ibid.*, p. 136.

[6] S. Radhakrishnan, *East and West* (New York: Harper and Brothers, 1956), p. 78. Used by permission of Harper and Row, Publishers, Inc.

[7] *Ibid.*, p. 73.

[8] Hendrik Kraemer, *Religion and the Christian Faith* (London: Lutterworth Press, 1956; Philadelphia: The Westminster Press, 1957), pp. 372–373. Used by permission of Lutterworth Press and The Westminster Press.

[9] For example, Henry James Forman and Roland Gammon, *Truth Is One, The Story of the World's Great Living Religions in Pictures and Text* (New York: Harper and Brothers, 1954), p. 6.

[10] Dr. Toynbee's views are set forth in various of his writings, especially the following: *A Study of History,* Vol. VII (New York: Oxford University Press, 1954); *An Historian's Approach to Religion* (New York: Oxford University Press, 1956); and *Christianity Among the Religions of the World* (New York: Charles Scribner's Sons, 1957).

[11] Arnold Toynbee, *Christianity Among the Religions of the World,* Preface. Used by permission of Charles Scribner's Sons.

[12] *Op. cit.*, pp. 129, 136.

[13] J. E. Lesslie Newbigin, *A Faith for This One World?* (New York: Harper and Brothers, 1961), pp. 45–46. Used by permission of Harper and Row, Publishers, Inc.

[14] Kraemer, *op. cit.*, pp. 251–252.

[15] Hendrik Kraemer, *The Christian Message in a Non-Christian World*, p. 128. Used by permission of Division of World Mission and Evangelism, World Council of Churches.

[16] *Ibid.*

Pronunciations

Adi Granth [AH-dee grunt]
Ahimsa [uh-HEEM-zuh]
Ahmadiyya [ah-mah-DEE-yah]
Ahura Mazda
   [AH-hoo-rah MAZ-dah]
Ainu [EYE-new]
a-jiva [ah-JEE-vuh]
Amidah [AH-mee-dah]
Angra Mainyu
   [AN-grah-mah-een-yoo]
animatism [AN-ih-may-tizm]
arahat [AH-rah-hut]
artha [UR-tah]
Arya Samaj [AHR-yuh sah-MAJ]
Baha'ism [bah-HAH-izm]
Bhagavad Gita
   [BUG-ah-vahd GEE-tah]
bhakti yoga [buck-te YOH-gah]
Bhave Vinoba
   [BAH-veh vee-NO-bah]
bodhisattva [boh-dee-SAT-vah]
Brahman [BRAH-man]
Brahmo Samaj
   [BRAH-mo sah-MAJ]
dharma [DAHR-mah]
Gautama [GAW-tuh-muh]
Hinayana [HEE-nah-YAH-nah]
Hindustan [HIN-do-stan]
Hokkaido [hoke-kah-ee-dough]
inao [ee-NAH-OH]
Jainism [JINE-izm]
jina [JEYE-nah]
jnana yoga [NYAH-nah YO-gah]
Kali [KAH-lee]
karma [KAHR-mah]
kiddush [KID-oosh]
Koran [kuh-RAHN]
Krishna [KRISH-nah]
Kshatriyas [KSHAH-tree-yah]
Mahabharata
   [mah-HAH-BAH-rah-tah]
Mahayana [MAH-hah-YAH-nah]

Medina [meh-DEE-nah]
Menorah [meh-NO-rah]
mezuzah [meh-ZOO-zah]
Mohammed [moh-HAH-met]
Nirvana [nur-VAH-nah]
Parseeism [PAHR-see-izm]
Pase Kamui
   [PAH-seh kah-MOO-ee]
Pesach [PAY-sahk]
Radhakrishnan
   [RAH-dah-KRISH-nun]
Ramadan [rah-mah-DAHN]
Ramakrishna
   [RAH-mah-KRISH-nuh]
Ramayana [rah-MAH-yah-nah]
Rigveda [rig-VAY-dah]
Rosh Hashanah
   [rohsh hah-SHAH-nah]
sadhu [SAH-due]
samsara [sahng-SAH-rah]
sannyasins [sun-NYAH-sins]
Sasaki [sa-SAH-ki]
shabuoth [sha-VOO-oath]
Shakti [SHUCK-tee]
Shema [she-MAH]
Shiites [SHE-itez]
Shiva [SHEE-vah]
Sikhs [SEEKS]
sindhu [SIN-doo]
Succoth [SUCK-uth]
Sunnis [SOON-eez]
Tagore Rabindranath
   [tah-GORE
   rah-BIN-drah-nath]
Taoism [DOW-izm]
Tao Te Ching [DOW-deh-JING]
Theravada [TEH-rah-vah-dah]
Vardhamana, Nataputta
   [var-dah-MAH-nah
   NAH-tuh-put-ah]
Vedanta [vay-DAHN-tah]
Vedas [VAY-duz]

Suggestions for the Teacher

THIS BOOK deals with a subject of vital interest and importance to American Christians. As never before, Christianity is face to face with the non-Christian religions. Christians need to know what these religions are and what is the Christian attitude toward them.

1. Defining the Teacher's Purpose

It is important that the teacher have clearly in mind his purpose in teaching the book. How about this for a statement of purpose? *To help the class member to have a basic understanding of the religions of the world and to have a Christian attitude toward these religions and those who profess them.*

2. Background Study

After reading the study book itself, it would be helpful to read a good general survey of world religions.

The World's Religions by Charles S. Braden, 1954 revised edition, Abingdon Press, $3.00 cloth, $1.25 paper, is a good survey book.

The World's Great Religions by R. E. Hume, 1959 revised edition, Scribner, $3.50, is perhaps the most helpful small book on the religions of the world.

The Religions of Mankind by E. D. Soper, 1951 revised edition, Abingdon, $3.50, is a larger survey book widely used as a college text.

It might be well to read a brief book on each of the major world religions. The series of small paperbacks by Friendship Press is very good: *Introducing Animism* by Nida and Smalley, *Introducing Buddhism* by Latourette, *Introducing Hinduism* by Pitt, and *Introducing Islam* by Wilson. The price is 90¢ each.

Helpful, also, is the inexpensive series published by Edinburgh House Press: *The Christian Approach to the Hindu* by Winslow, *The Christian Approach to the Jew* by Ellison, *The Christian Approach to the Buddhist* by Appleton, and *The Christian Approach to the Muslim* by Marrison. *Our Jewish Neighbors* (now out of print) by Frank Halbeck, published by the Baptist Home Mission Board, will admirably supplement the material of chapter 5.

World Within a World by Elwyn Means (6c), 85¢, is an excellent discussion of the Moslem World to supplement chapter 7.

Perhaps some of these books can be procured from your church, school, or public library, from the Baptist Book Store, or from your pastor.

3. *Ideas for Vital Discussion*

(1) Bring contemporary materials into use: visual aids, newspaper and magazine articles, and the like. For example, some articles on Zen Buddhism or Black Islam might give added interest to the material of the book on these subjects. *The Commission* and *Home Missions* may yield useful information. Also, the Home Mission Board has tracts on Jewish evangelism. Inquire about free literature on Vedanta Hinduism from Ramakrishna-Vivekananda Center, 17 East 94th Street, New York City; on Zen Buddhism from The First Zen Institute of America, Inc., 113 East 30th Street, New York 16, N.Y.; and on Baha'ism from the Baha'i Publishing Trust, 110 Linden Avenue, Wilmette, Illinois.

(2) A visit of the class (or at least the teacher) to a Jewish synagogue, a Baha'i meeting place, or a Vedanta Center, should prove profitable and interesting, if possible of arrangement.

(3) Participation in the class discussion by a missionary to people of the particular religion studied should lend interest and a touch of realism to the study. Participation by representatives of the religions involved might even be better.

(4) In some cases, the assigning of reports to members of the class might encourage more individual study and participation.

(5) Raise thought-provoking questions. For instance, on chapter 9 you might pose this problem: Suppose you were a missionary to Japan, and one of your converts should say to you, "I am so grateful for what God has done for me in Christ. But my grandmother never heard of Jesus. Although she was a Buddhist, her character seemed like that of a Christian. Now, must I believe that she is suffering eternal punishment?" How would you answer? Why?

4. *Visual Aids*

Desire of All Nations. A Broadman filmstrip prepared especially to accompany CHRISTIANITY AND WORLD RELIGIONS and *Missions Today.* Gives historical background and strength of major religions of the world and the challenge they present to Christianity. 45 frames, color, manual. $6.00.

The Challenge of the Moslem World. A graphic presentation of the Christian responsibility to share the gospel with the millions of the Moslem world. 64 frames, color, manual. (7f) $3.50.

Judaism Today. History, worship, and major holidays. Brotherhood exemplified by 4 chaplains who gave up life jackets when ship *Dorchester* sank. 32 frames, color. (53-s) $6.00.

Islam Today. History and contemporary aspects and beliefs. 30 frames, color. (53-s) $6.00.

Buddhism Today. Characteristics and development. 34 frames, color. (53-s) $6.00.

Hinduism Today. Hinduism's many gods, carrying ideas, seemingly conflicting beliefs. 42 frames, color. (53-s) $6.00.

For Review and Written Work

CHAPTER 1

1. How would you define "religion"?
2. Is religion universal?
3. What is "secularism"?
4. What are some examples of religious revival in today's world?

CHAPTER 2

5. What is meant by "primitive people"?
6. What are the general characteristics of primitive religion?
7. What are some of the problems in Christianity's relation to people of primitive culture today?

CHAPTER 3

8. Why is Hinduism so hard to define or describe?
9. Does Hinduism offer more than one way of salvation? Explain.
10. Give a brief description of the caste system of Hinduism.
11. What is the challenge of Vedanta to the Christian faith?

CHAPTER 4

12. How did Buddhism originate?
13. Compare and contrast the two branches of Buddhism: Theravada and Mahayana.
14. Discuss the missionary revival of Buddhism.
15. Why is Zen popular among some people in America and Europe?

CHAPTER 5

16. What are the fundamental concepts of Chinese religion?
17. How does Confucianism differ from Taoism?
18. Describe Chinese popular religion.
19. What are the prospects for the continued existence and growth of religion in Communist China?

CHAPTER 6

20. Describe the Jewish attitude toward the sabbath.
21. Why is the course of Jewish history a "tragic" one?
22. What are the main types of Judaism? How are they distinguished from each other?
23. What should be the Christian attitude toward the Jew?

CHAPTER 7

24. What is your impression of Mohammed?
25. What are the basic beliefs of Islam?
26. Discuss the missionary revival of Islam.
27. Describe the "Black Muslims."

CHAPTER 8

28. How has Shinto, as a primitive religion, managed to survive in a highly educated nation?
29. Discuss the monotheism of Zoroaster.
30. How does Jainism differ from Buddhism?
31. In what ways was Sikhism a synthesis?
32. What are the main teachings of Baha'ism?

CHAPTER 9

33. What is the Christian concept of tolerance?
34. Do you believe that there is "general revelation"? How is this related to the revelation in Christ?
35. What should be the Christian attitude toward other religions?